STRANGERS AMONG US

Louise Clamme and Sinuard Castelo

authorHOUSE®

AuthorHouse™
1663 Liberty Drive
Bloomington, IN 47403
www.authorhouse.com
Phone: 1-800-839-8640

First published by AuthorHouse 9/14/2011

ISBN: 978-1-4634-3174-7 (e)
ISBN: 978-1-4634-3175-4 (dj)
ISBN: 978-1-4634-3176-1 (sc)

Library of Congress Control Number: 2011911970

Printed in the United States of America

Acknowledgements

This has been a long-overdue project to give credit to those immigrants who contributed to the growth and economic development of Blackford County, Indiana, when gas and oil were discovered here in the late 19th century. There was a new courthouse and brick business blocks were being built around the square. In the immigrants' eyes there was the dream to come to a "new land" and have the opportunity for a better life for themselves and their families.

The book is a compilation of information gathered from newspapers of the day, court documents, and advertisements of the time highlighting those strangers by language and customs that came to the County. There is no doubt that many who contributed went about their daily activities or left to seek work elsewhere. Such information is long gone. We could only document what we could find but hope it is enough to let our community in 2010 understand a little better those"strangers" who came before us and the mark they left in our county.

Truly, America was a "melting pot" and our small community proves that.

Special thanks to Don Rogers for his help with pictures and Mary Lou Marshall for technical support.

Louise Clamme and Sinuard Castelo

2010

South Side of Hartford City Square. The frame buildings on this side of the square were to be torn down and all brick buildings to be erected. The "removal sale" was in progress. Date: May 10, 1893.

The Stranger Among Us Foreword

Long before Horace Greely printed his sage advice to "Go West, young man, go West!" many men young and old, were moving west. Not only second, third and fourth generation Americans were moving ever westward, but the people of Europe and Asia felt the call to "go west." America became the symbol of hope, of freedom, of unlimited opportunities. Wars, famine, religious persecution and diminishing land space for farming pushed thousands to seek America's riches.

Immigration was a tough decision for families to make. Although they loved the fatherland and bitterly hated the thought of possibly never seeing their beloved relatives again, they bravely packed up and started westward across the broad Atlantic toward a new life filled with rose-colored dreams.

Little by little, hardy souls ventured into Indiana, the 19th state, to establish their homes and found their communities. The first settlers, the Reasoner families, came into Blackford County as early as 1831. The County was organized in 1839, third smallest in the state. Slowly the great trees were felled and miles of tile laid in the ground to drain the wet and marshy land. The first settlers were largely Germans, central Europeans, sturdy hard-working agriculturists. Many of them plied a second trade on the side such as shoe making, blacksmithing, canery, school teaching and preaching. The merchants, millers, tavern keepers, doctors, and lawyers followed close in their wake.

For many years the County slowly and peacefully expanded. Many young men married the girl who lived just down the road and raised their large families near their parents and grandparents. Some of the County's young men opted to go on farther west where the great expanses of Iowa, Kansas, Nebraska, the Dakotas held out alluring promises of rich and fertile farms land.

Then gas and oil were discovered! That precious fuel, drawn from the earth almost effortlessly, changed the County and its population within a few months. Almost overnight, life seemed to go from quiet, peaceful and unhurried to bustling excitement, hurrying and scurrying, the air filled with the booms of exploding nitroglycerine. The cheapness of the fuel attracted manufacturing, especially glass making which required very high heat to melt and fuse its components into workable product. At one time in the very early 20th century, there were thirteen glass factories in the County. Some existed only a short time, some produced for many years. The County also had two large paper mills, a spoke factory, tile mills, feed mills, and smaller enterprises

Manufacturing requires labor, and laboring men soon came. Some were artisans, masters of their trades; many were unskilled, untrained; each necessary in his special way.

The Belgians and the French, glassmen in their native lands, were the largest foreign-born segment in the County. They clustered on the south side of Hartford City, south of Little Lick Creek, although the 1900 census lists several living in Montpelier. At first there was little association between the local residents and the strangers in their midst, as is to be expected, but this reticense changed after a while as the immigrants strove to make themselves more "American."

Alas, the gas did not last forever as expected and manufacturers no longer sought Blackford County as a desirable location. The Great Depression of the 1930's took its toll on the County as it did all over the nation.

During both the good and the lean years, immigrants continued to come to little Blackford County, some for a short time, some to live out their lives in this place and at last rest in the earth of this County.

In these pages are the stories of some of the strangers who came to this part of America to add their influence in shaping the legacy of the County's interesting history.

A need for building materials and an abundance of native timber provided jobs for many. In these two pictures large trees were being hauled to local sawmills.

Horse drawn log wagons

Table of Contents

THE BELGIANS
AND THE FRENCH

Larmoyeux Pierre Campbell blk
Martin & Fargo New Smith blk
McGeath M H Campbell blk
Rhoades & Spence Cooley blk
Rife & Hummer Vancieve blk

LIFE

Metropolitan J L Lance assistant supt Weiler blk
Prudential 217½ w Wash New Smith blk

RESTAURANTS

Blount J M 118 e Wash
Home Restaurant Jno Blake prop 114 n Jeff
Hubartt J V basement Carrell blk
James W W 118 s Jeff
Legros Alfred 605 w Wash

New Era S L Mocts prop 107 n High
Pursley M J 517 w Wash
Roberts E M 233 w Wash

SALOONS

Abbott & Saxon (The Bank) 116 n Jeff
Andre Ursmar 1319 s Monroe
Arcade Saloon Mrs Salrin prop 1506-1508 s Jeff
Berrian August Jeff and Sheridan
Dandoy Chas 100 e Seventh
Diamond Saloon 123 e Fifth
Eagle Saloon Jeff and Seventh
Hoster Cafe e Wash
Ingram Bar Hotel Ingram blk
Kentucky Liquor Co 117 w Wash
Kraus J 115 n High
Logansport Saloon J. B. Dumont prop w Cleveland st
Lake Erie Saloon e Wash
Mitchell Pat 123 w Wash
Mondron Leon Fifth and Monroe
Patoux Desire w Wash opp Panhandle frt sta

J.L.Hoover

Red Onion Saloon Fred Meaise prop w end Water
Russell Lewis 108 e Wash
Ryan B F 116½ n Jeff
Schweier Emil opp Johnston Glass factory
Steffey Corb e Wash
South Side Casino Joe Quinet prop 216-218 e Seventh
The Mecca 114 w Main
Union Saloon west Wash

SECOND HAND STORES

Culberson L B 303 w Wash
Noah's Ark M M Dickey prop 200 n Jeff

SHOEMAKERS AND REPAIRERS

Brown E M 121 n High
Cronin James upstairs Citizens State Bank blk

Gottschalk E E 109 w Wash
Schisler J M 212 w Main

STEAMSHIP AGENTS

Garvey & Berger office upstairs in Campbell blk

STEAM DYE WORKS

Wilson Jno S 200½ w Main

TELEGRAPH COMPANIES

Western Union Telegraph Co Geo O Brown mgr 117½ w Wash

TELEPHONE COMPANIES

United Telephone Co Vancleve blk
Central Union Telephone Co upstairs Dick blk

UNDERTAKERS

Bell W H 211 n High
Cox & Baxter 215 w Wash

VETERINARY

Anderson F W office Walnut street between Main and Wash

J. L. Hoover

Very young work force probably glass workers.

Glass Factory laborers. Note the young boys in the picture. Often they were sent to the saloons to get buckets of beer for the glassworkers.

George Turner hauled for the Indianapolis Brewing Company. In this photo he is delivering to another saloon on the South Side.

George Turner standing by wagon at the Diamond Saloon located at the corner of Monroe and Fifth Street.

J. Berger was an agent for the Indianapolis Brewing Company. He appears here in the dark suit and George Turner. Deliveryman, is on his left with his arm on the wagon.

A group of glassworkers on the South Side.

Glassworkers on the job. Only Raymond Lyle, a Mr. Briscoe, and a person bearing the initials of T. C. are identified.

Charles Dandoy's saloon advertisement for his business located on the South Side. His business was in operation in 1906.   Dandoys immigrated from Belgium.

East Washington Street also featured its share of saloons; The Old Reliable Saloon was operated by Mr. Dumont, an immigrant from Belgium.

*In 1906 Skeeter's Barber Shop offered first class work
to all citizens of Blackford County.*

Glass factory workers around 1900.

The workforce in Blackford County

With the discovery of gas and oil in East Central Indiana in the late 1880's, the glass factories were attracted to the area because of the cheap fuel needed to produce the high temperatures necessary in making glass. Men in Belgium and northern France had been making glass for centuries and their skills were passed down from generation to generation. Suddenly, this vast new area, America, needed their expertise. Unmarried men and whole families were soon making the long and tiring voyage across the wide Atlantic, and then on west to Indiana.

In Blackford County, third smallest in the state, the immigrants found employment at the Hartford City Glass Company, (later known as the American Window Glass Company), second largest glass factory in the United States, as well as other smaller factories in the area. The glass workers lived near the huge plant situated south of Hartford City which soon became known as the South Side. As nearly as possible, the Belgian and French peoples clung to the old ways which they had known in the homeland. But slowly they became a drop in the "melting pot" of America.

The following excerpts from local newspapers record some of the happenings in the daily life of the Belgian and French people as they slowly became Americans.

Telegram   September 28, 1893

A TALE OF A FRENCH BAKER

Joseph Mommerts, the French baker of the South Side, sold his bakery and his horse and wagon to Leopold Shaller and quietly departed for Jeanette, Pennsylvania where he will enter up the same business.

The above is an ordinary news item, but the "whys" and "wherefores" are what make up an interesting bit about Joseph. He was an energetic and businesslike fellow, and a money maker. It wasn't poor trade that drove

11

him from Hartford City. It may all be attributed to domestic relations, which had been anything but comfortable for the past five weeks. It was about that time that his wife arrived from Belgium, and found just what she expected, her husband living with her sister as his wife. She had telegraphed to Joseph to look for her on a certain train. Joseph met her at the depot and escorted her to his home on the hill, where everybody embraced and looked happy. There was no hair pulling, no gnashing of teeth, no deep tragedy at the meeting. The wife did not like the usurpation but she remained cool. She may have started from home mad as a hornet, but a long voyage across the water and many miles of bumping car travel had sweetened her disposition.

Three years earlier Mommerts and his wife had settled at Jeanette where he built up a splendid business. His wife grew discontented and pined for the old country. Finally Joseph sold everything at a sacrifice and went back with her. But he was not satisfied and concluded that America was the place to make money. His wife refusing to accompany him, he took her sister and came over and located in Hartford City. Everything had gone smoothly until the arrival of Mrs. Mommerts. It took five weeks to dispel that false impression. Mr. and Mrs. Mommerts agreed to a mutual separation and drew up papers to that effect, Joseph paying over $300. He went to Jeanette to try to build up his business again. There he hoped to get a divorce from his wife and marry her sister.

Evening News   February 23, 1894

Adolph Wuchner, proprietor of the Midway Café, is the possessor of a meerschaum pipe by which he sets great store. Yesterday the pipe was missed. Wuchner suspected a hanger-on about the place and told him he would give him $10 if he would find it. The fellow went away but pretty soon returned with the pipe. He refused to tell where he got the missing meerschaum and Marshal Butler arrested him on Adolph's complaint. The man was taken Squire Edson's office and left in charge of Adolph while the Marshal went in search of the prosecutor. But Adolph proved a careless guard and the alleged thief slipped out the back and made his escape. Adolph has his pipe and is disposed to regard the thief's escape as a joke.

<u>Evening News</u>   March 2, 1894

The Belgians living on the South Side had a celebration yesterday. They had heard from the conscription returns in Belgium and such of those who had not taken out naturalization papers here were jubilant, so they can return to their homes without being compelled to do duty in the army. They got out a band, serenaded the neighbors and had a good time generally.

<u>Telegram</u>   March 5, 1894

Emile Jacart, for a long time employed by John Berger as bartender and driver of his beer wagon, died rather suddenly yesterday, and although complaining of feeling unwell, did not seem uneasy about his condition. He got shaved at the barber shop and went home. About noon he sent for a doctor, who found him breathing painfully. He had previously pulled through several such spells and it was thought he would recover from this one. Jacart was very popular with those who knew him and his death is sincerely regretted.

<u>Evening News</u>   March 5, 1894

The Belgian Dramatic Society will produce the French play, "La Tache de Sang," at Dogneaux's Hall, South Side, next Saturday evening. This drama is in three acts and will be given by the Society in good style. Everybody should avail themselves of the opportunity of seeing a French play. Admission 10 and 15 cents.

<u>Evening News</u>   March 16, 1894

The wedding of Mr. Ellie Lefevre and Miss Adelilna Lariaux was made the occasion of an elaborate celebration at the residence of the bride's parents, Mr. and Mrs. Antoine Lariaux, on the South Side. The ceremony was performed by Squire Kearny shortly after 8 o'clock in the evening, and the company once sat down to a banquet that lasted from 8:30 until after 2 o'clock. The eatables provided were tremendous in quantity and the guests only quit feasting when they could feast no more. Between the courses there was singing and the Squire, as an honored guest, felt called upon to contribute his voice to the entertainment. He sang "The Star Spangled

Banner" in a style that he had never equaled before and was unanimously voted out of sight. During the festivities Mr. Auguste Collett and Miss Eugenie Lariaux, another daughter of the host and hostess, announced their intention to get married next week, when another season of festivities will be indulged in. The Lariaux family is a prolific one. At the banquet, ten married children were present.

Evening News   March 27, 1894

Miss Martha Gaillard of the South Side will be married to Mr. Emile Andre of Gas City. The bride is a handsome Belgian maiden who has been employed at Martin's Hotel for the past year. The groom is a well known glass gatherer, who formerly worked for the Hartford City Glass Company. A large number of friends from this city will attend the wedding ceremony. A reception will follow accompanied with the lively time that Belgians appreciate.

Telegram   June 24, 1895

A SMALL PANIC AT THE CATHOLIC CHURCH

There was a small sized panic at the Catholic Church yesterday morning, but the outcome was fortunate, no one being injured. The church was crowded to witness the first communion services. There were forty-one children to receive their first communion, by far the largest class in the history of the church in this city. Just as the children were marching out of the sanctuary before receiving communion, the veil of Mary Rectonus, of Dunkirk, one of the communicants, caught fire from another little girl's candle. There was a flash and the veil was immediately thrown to the floor and extinguished. The audience were at once panic stricken and only those in front knew of the lucky termination of the accident. There was intense excitement for several minutes. Several persons jumped through a window, while others rushed about frantically. One young lady, Miss Mary McGrawl, jumped through a down stairs window with one bound and completely ruined Father Dhe's bean patch. However, the whole affair ended so fortunately that the reverend gentleman is glad to know that the garden was the only thing damaged.

Telegram   May 10, 1899

Glass men are not more convivial than are the workmen in other trades, and a compilation of the beverages sold on the South Side shows that they have a large assortment from which to choose. Here are some of the popular drinks indulged in by the foreign-born workmen: Absinthe, Bitter Absinthe, Raspail, Cognac, Rhum, Haslet, Vieux Systome, Crème de Noyaux, Eau de Vie, Kummel, Anisette, Eau de Argent and Eau de Or.

Telegram   November 20, 1901

AMONG THE WEST END FACTORY MEN

The west end of Hartford City has enjoyed a phenomenal growth the past year not only as a factory district but as a resident section as well. The factories of the Johnston Glass Company, Blackford Glass Company, National Rolling Mill, Sans Pariel Glass Company, American Window Glass's No. 32 and Clelland Glass Company are all clustered together between railway switches and driveways, making it a busy place. Building of business rooms and dwellings is still going on there.

The glass at the Blackford is first class and all the blowers have a full quota of boxes.

The glass at the Johnston tank is improving and it will not be long until it will be silver clear and devoid of the occasional stones that have caused some annoyance heretofore. Fortune Dogneaux is one of the very best master teasers in the country and he can be depended upon to bring them out all right. (A master teaser was the man who saw that the ingredients for making glass were mixed correctly.)

Evening News   June 23, 1902

The wedding of Frank Schmidt, son of Gus Schmidt, and Irma Brasseur, daughter of Gaspard Brasseur, which was solemnized at the Catholic Church this morning at 10 o'clock, was the prettiest church wedding that has taken place in this part of the state this year.

All the costumes worn were splendid and the ceremony which was conducted by Father Dhe, was the same impressive and beautiful one that is usually used by the Catholics for weddings.

After the ceremony the young couple were given a dinner at the home of the bride's parents on the South Side and all the friends and immediate relatives participated.

Mr. Schmidt is a gatherer in the American factory No. 3, and the young couple will make their home with the bride's parents until fall.

Evening News   July 17, 1903

WOMEN CARRY FAMILY PURSE

The Belgian Women Make Allowances to Their Husbands and Invest the Money

The club women who are discussing their right to a share of the contents of the husband's pocketbook are divided on the question how much they should take. How large should their allowance be? Ten percent, say some, five percent say others; still others say the percentage should vary according to the cost of living in different localities. But it is admitted by all the women who fondly believe they are advance thinkers that they should have an allowance which would remove the necessity for asking the family provider for money every time they desired to go down town to make the most trifling purchase.

Our Belgian fellow citizens have solved the question in a manner that would be eminently satisfactory to the native woman, although her husband would doubtless object more strenuously than she does under similar conditions. The Belgian woman carries the pocketbook and she makes the allowance to her husband instead of the husband to her. The Belgian woman in this city pursues the same methods in this country that she did in the old country. She makes the family purchases, even to buying the clothes for her husband and grownup sons. She does the marketing and she is a shrewd buyer. The consequence of this is that there is something generally laid up in a Belgian family for the rainy day that comes to most families some time or other in their existence.

Among the dwellers in Hartford City there are no more thrifty families than the Belgian families. The husbands take their wages home—although it is on record that some of the tricky ones will "knock down" on their wives by deceiving them as to the amount of their earnings—and the good wife puts it away where she thinks it will do the most good. If the wages are much in excess of the living expenses it will not be long before she will have an account in a bank. A banker told an Evening News reporter some time ago that the public would be surprised if it knew how many of the Belgian residents carried balances in the banks.

The Belgian families here are notably thrifty and it is attributed to the fact that the women carry the pocketbook and control the expenditures. The heads of the families have been brought up in the belief that the wife is the proper custodian of their earnings and they are inclined to look with pity not unmixed with contempt on the improvidence of American workmen who themselves carry the pocketbook into places where they are tempted to spend its contents.

<u>Telegram</u>　　　　　August, 1903

NO MORE SOUTH SIDE CARNIVAL HERE

For the first time in twelve years there will be no carnival by the window glassworkers in this city this season.

After the erection of the third largest window glass plant in the world in the city, the French and Belgian workers began holding an annual carnival, which served as a sort of reunion for them, and people of these two nationalities traveled hundreds of miles to renew and cement a friendship formed in the old country.

When these carnivals were first given the people here, unaccustomed to the French and Belgian methods of entertainment, made vigorous protest against the wholesale and retail consumption of beer, but after two or three carnivals nothing was thought of it.

Notwithstanding the vast amount of beer consumed, no French or Belgian was ever seen intoxicated while more than one American citizen caused trouble and was arrested.

The absorption of the big window glass plant by the trust has had the effect of doing away with the annual entertainment. Following the introduction of blowing machines, there has been a general exodus of French and Belgian workmen. No less than five co-operative companies have been formed here within the past three months, and the Belgians and French are leaving in large numbers. The South Side, once known as the Belgian colony, numbering 2,000 people, is almost deserted by them. Many are selling their property for less than half it cost, in their eagerness to get away. It seems to be the desire of the Belgians to put as much distance between them and the blowing machine as possible. No greater insult could be offered to one of these men than try to employ him to run a blowing machine.

17

<u>Evening News</u>   December 17, 1907

GUSTAVE WILLAUME DIES SUDDENLY
AT MAUMEE, OHIO

Gustave Willaume, one of early Belgium residents of Hartford City dropped dead at Maumee, Ohio.

Willaume was 57 years of age and a member of the Amalgamated Association. He was a blower and one of the best in the business. He became a resident of this city when the Hartford City Glass Company erected the Southside plant and lived here until two years ago. Three sons and a daughter also survive.

<u>Daily Times Gazette</u>   October 15, 1908

WILHEMS FIRES WILLMAN BLOCK

Bart Wilhems startled the city Wednesday night in two highly original acts, such are put on only by Bart.

The first was setting fire to the Willman block, where he had pre-empted a room and second was being hustled down stairs and through a crowd of several hundred with nothing on but an abbreviated sweater.

It was shortly before 7 o'clock when smoke was seen pouring out of the second story of the Willman block above the Schlitz buffet. Investigation showed that the fire was blazing in a room with the door locked. When an entrance was forced the floor was found afire and in the center quite a hole had been burned. The whole floor was ablaze but the actual fire was extinguished with but little water. The damage to the ceiling by water is probably greater than the direct fire loss.

While the fire was blazing Bart was discovered in a bed, locked in a front room and, although the smoke was so thick it could be cut, he refused to get out, pleading his lack of raiment. Marshal Worley with the assistance of bystanders forcibly dragged him downstairs and into the back room of the saloon. His appearance in the crowd with so little clothing on created more than a sensation. Bart was put in a back room and told to stay there while Marshal Worley hunted up some clothing for him. When he returned Bart had disappeared in the alley and was not found for about an hour. Night Policeman Byars picked him up wandering around still clothed in his shrunken sweater. Bart was placed in jail and the officers hunted up a few more garments so he was at least safe from the charge of public indecency. It is likely John Willman, who owns the building, will file charges against him.

From what Bart says it appears setting fire to the building was not a deliberate act but just a piece of his carelessness. Bart had been occupying the back room but was ejected a few days ago on order of John Willman. Bart went out and then came right back again. Wednesday evening he had removed his garments in the back room, except for the high water sweater, then lit his pipe and threw the match down on the floor that was littered with papers and calmly marched off to the front room to sleep. That the fire was not intentional was evidenced by the fact that part of Bart's own wardrobe was burned.

One reason Willman recently ordered Bart out was that Wilhems was making a mushroom bed in one of the empty rooms in the block and had been carrying manure from a livery stable to make the mushrooms grow. The owner of the building did not care to have Bart around anyhow but the mushroom business was the last straw.

Hartford City News-Times   November 23, 1940

FIVE BELGIAN RESIDENTS GRANTED CITIZENSHIP

"God – bless America!"

That was the supplication voiced through tears of happiness by one of five Blackford County residents—all natives of Belgium—who were granted their final citizenship papers in the Blackford circuit court.

Those receiving their final naturalization papers, entitling them to the rights of American citizenship, were Mrs. Laura Lambiott, 70: Mrs. Julia DePalma, 65; Fred DeVilles, 58; Leon Pettit, 66; and Arthur Pettit, 64.

For the five who took their oaths of allegiance to the Stars and Stripes, it was a happy occasion. Some choked back tears, others shed tears unashamed—but all voiced their happiness in terms that bespoke their patriotic fervor and love for America.

Judge W. A. Burns presided over the court of naturalization, with E. J. Scantland, of Cincinnati, serving as the examiner for the Department of Justice. As each applicant was called before the court, both the federal examiner and Judge Burns questioned them closely.

Through the entire hearing, listening closely to all proceedings, were members of the D. A. R., the American Legion and Elks Lodge. Then as the court rendered its decision, granting the five their rights of American citizenship, all stood at attention—hands over their hearts—as the Oath of Allegiance was administered.

Mrs. Howard Ervin, acting for the Nancy Knight chapter of the D. A. R., extended a welcome to the newly-made citizens and presented each of them a manual of citizenship.

Jack Dolan, a past commander of the Paul Moyer American Legion Post, then gave to each of the five people small silk American flags, presented to the Legion for this purpose by the Elks Lodge.

Pent-up, anxious emotions of the newly-made citizens broke under the friendly greetings of the three organizations, and as they accepted the small silk flags, they gave voice separately to their feelings: "God—bless America!" came from the lips of Mrs. Julia DePalma, who had just told court officials that she had two sons in World War I.

"It's my flag now—thank God!" was the response of Fred DeVilles as he reverently took his small silk flag. And from the others came like expressions—voiced separately, tears welling in their eyes—not tears of regret or sadness in renouncing the land of their birth, but those of happiness which words could not express.

"It's Thanksgiving time—I am truly thankful," said Mrs. Laura Lambiott. "I came to America when I was six years old—I have only known one country—my America," said Leon Pettit, who had one son in World War I. "It's my America now!"

It was the ceremony of its kind ever held by patriotic organizations in a court of naturalization here, to welcome newly-made citizens. The groups represented at the hearing gave an atmosphere that was highly impressive.

The questions of the examiner and the court pertained not only to the lives of the applicants, but to matters of civil government, to ascertain the qualifications of each person as they faced citizenship.

Each was asked where he or she was born, when they came to America, how long they had resided in Blackford County and whether their parents had applied for, or been granted naturalization. The questions pertained to civil government, based on the Constitution, the three branches of government, namely executive, legislative and judicial, the method of electing a president, the difference between a democracy and a monarchy or totalitarian form of government, the Bill of Rights, how laws are made, the number of Senators and Congressmen, state government, and kindred questions.

The concluding question was whether they were willing to renounce the land of their birth, swear allegiance to the United States, and whether they would serve and protect this country by individual sacrifice if called upon.

One applicant, the mother of two sons who were in the first World War, made prompt answer to the question: "I gave my only two sons, not knowing whether they would come back. I was willing then, and I'm willing now to do anything I can for this country—for my country."

Mrs. Lambiott said she had visited the land of her birth in 1938, and had returned to America to spend the remainder of her life. She said she had lived in this vicinity for some fifty years. Character witnesses were Mrs. Rosa Gilbert and Mrs. Zoe Suain..

Mrs. DePalma said she had come to America from Belgium when she was nine years of age and had lived in Blackford County for over forty-seven years. Her character witnesses were William Hess and Mrs. Rosa Gilbert.

Fred DeVillez said he came to Blackford County in 1893, coming to America in 1884. His witnesses were Clarence Pattison and Henry Blake.

Leon Pettit said he came to America when he was six years of age. He had a son in the first World War. His character witnesses were August Young and Edward Cox.

Arthur Pettit said he had come to Blackford County in 1889. His character witnesses were Robert Bonham and Floyd Huffman.

Legionaires and D. A. R. members congratulated each of the five new citizens individually, and the reactions were both kindly and appreciative.

"This is the happiest day of my life," one of the newly-made women citizens said. "I want to frame my silk flag and keep it forever."

LOCAL MAN BORN IN BELGIUM
PROFESSED LOVE FOR AMERICA

American culture has been enriched through the years by the customs and character of immigrants to our shores, whether those immigrants came to this country while we were still a colony of England, or during the years since we have grown to become a world power.

Leon LeClercq, who died August 24, 1959, in Hartford City, was one such person who emigrated to this country from Belgium in 1891, and for 68 years helped in the growth of the new country which he adopted.

Shortly before the death of Mr. LeClercq, his wife discovered a letter which he had written to his grandson and adopted son, Paul, telling of his heritage and his feelings for his adopted country. The sentiments expressed by Mr. LeClercq are such that many could benefit from reading them, so his widow has given permission for the letter to be reproduced for all to read.

Hartford City, Indiana
January 14, 1954

In order that my grandson, Paul LeClercq, will know where his grandfather came from, I, Leon Amie LeClercq, was born in Charleroi, Belgium on April 14, 1876, the son of Francois Gilain LeClercq, and of Celina Augustine Bricault. I remember when I was six years old the family moved to France in a town called Mauberege. I went to school there for three years, then we moved back to Belgium when I was nine years old, to the same town.

There I went to school for three more years, and when I was 13 years old I went to work in the glass factory. I was shove-in boy, as they called us. I worked there two years, 12 hours a day for several days a week, and received one franc a day. That is about 20 cents in our money. That was in 1890 and late in December of that year we came to America, landing in New York in 1891. We were days crossing the water, and then we went to Jeanette, Pennsylvania, to work in the glass factory.

We were six at home now, three boys and one girl and father and mother. We all worked in the factory except mother and sister at home, and we were happy in America. It was just like Heaven to us all. That was in 1891, now in 1954 America is still like Heaven to us all.

Father, like the rest of us, wanted to become an American, so the first thing he did was to apply for his first citizenship papers, which he received in 1891. He got his first papers at the county seat of Greenburg, in that year.

We lived in Jeanette two years, then we moved to Dunkirk, Indiana, in 1893, where father applied for his second citizenship papers, and got them. That made me an American too, because I was only 17 years old. I still have my father's papers today.

Now Paul, we are in June, 1953. I am now 77 years old, and this is my week before retiring from the Johnston Glass company, and America is still a Heaven to us all.

From your Grandfather,
Leon Amie LeClercq

FATHER DHE

Prior to Father Dhe's coming, the Catholics in Hartford City were a small group with assets of one small frame building, indebtedness of $84 and no priest. With the coming of the Belgian and French glassmen, nearly all Catholics, the need became even greater. The congregation was delighted when in 1896 Father Charles Dhe was assigned to the local church. He spoke very little English, but with diligent study, in a few months he was able to deliver his sermon in English.

He was the first and foremost a man of God, dedicated to his calling. His parishioners were most dear to him, rejoicing with them in happy times, sharing their sorrows in times of adversity.

A handsome new church, St. John The Evangelist, was dedicated April 24, 1898 and later a parochial residence, a school and a sisters' residence were added. Besides the congregation in Hartford City, Father Dhe had churches in Montpelier and Dunkirk. In both these places, churches were built about the same time where increasing membership attested to Father Dhe's energy and unceasing toil.

In addition to being a priest and a builder, Father Dhe was a practical and knowledgeable business man. Since many of his parishioners were glass workers, he was interested in glass making in all its forms. He was owner-manager of the National Window Glass factory in Montpelier, established in 1899 and sold in 1904. Father Dhe was president of the Sans Pareil glass factory located on the west side of Hartford City which closed in 1901 after only a year in production.

In September 1906 Father Dhe was sent to Fowler, Indiana, to minister to Sacred Heart church there. He died June 14, 1939.

During his twelve years in Hartford City, Father Dhe's influence was felt in the church and the community. He had friends wherever he went who grieved when he left Hartford City and they visited the beloved priest as often as possible at Fowler.

GLASSWORKERS' HEADQUARTERS
___SALOON___

EMIL SCHWEIER, PROPRIETOR

Phone 251 - Residence Phone 329

HARTFORD CITY, INDIANA

The   South   Side   Saloon

___Corner Seventh and Jefferson Streets___
Fine Wines, Liquors and Cigars.
Cool, refreshing Beer always on
tap. Don't forget to call on Charley
when you visit the South Side.

CHARLES DANDOY, PROPRIETOR

Hartford City, Indiana

BELGIANS APPLYING FOR CITIZENSHIP IN BLACKFORD COUNTY

Name	Date of Arrival
Aigrisse, Alfred	September 19, 1893
Andre, Joseph	August 27, 1899
Andris, Louis	September 11, 1893
Aussecruer, Arthur	November 29, 1892
Ayrisse, Jean Baptiste	October 7, 1900
Bagot, Fernand	February 14, 1907
Bandouin, Joseph	August 15, 1893
Bastin, Eugene	April 20, 1898
Bastin, Joseph	November 15, 1900
Bastine, Louis	September 1, 1893
Bauthiere, Arthur	August 29, 1893
Beaudoux, George	September 23, 1893
Berger, Edmond	December 23, 1906
Berger, Nicholas	February 5, 1895
Berger, Urbain	August 29, 1893
Beria, Alphonzo	August 20, 1891
Bertaux, Edmond	November 17, 1888
Borley, Leon	September 10, 1901
Bormans, Hubert	November 19, 1892
Bormans, John	November 19, 1892
Bormans, John	November 19, 1892
Bormans, Joseph	November 13, 1891
Botmans, Lou	November 11, 1892
Boucher, Antoine	December 18, 1880
Boulanger, Joseph	November, 1899
Bouvier, Louis	October 10, 1893
Brasseuer, Virgile	August 23, 1893
Brasseur, Albert	September 6, 1890
Brasseur, Emile	October 15, 1893
Brasseur, Gaspard	September 6, 1890
Buulenger, Joseph	November, 1899
Cabaret, Emile	August 20, 1893
Carena, Bernard	August 25, 1900
Clement, Leopold	September, 1882
Collet, Eloi	December 15, 1900
Colletts, August	June, 1890
Cormil, Oscar	October 7, 1901

Cornil, Emile	September 4, 1893
Courtin, Marcelin	March 21, 1892
Dandoy, Arthur	September 25, 1900
Darvenne, Joseph	November, 1886
Debruyn, Herman	September 5, 1889
Deffet, Desire	August 29, 1893
Delaisse, Joseph	May 3, 1893
Delbart, Auguste	November 3, 1905
Delbart, Jenius	September 15, 1905
Delporte, Aime	July 1, 1891
Delporte, Desire	November 3, 1893
Demeester, Adrian	March 12, 1896
Deriep, Altor	October 12,, 1893
Desgain, Hector	October, 1891
Desgain, Jules	October 5, 1893
Dethier, Alfred	November 3, 1888
Devillez, Leopold	July 9, 1886
Dewez, Florentine	September 3, 1892
Dewez, Valantin	September 21, 1893
Doffinez, August	September 12, 1900
Dognaux, Martial	October 4, 1898
Dourlet, Nestor	September 17, 1890
Dressart, Edmond	August 5, 1893
Duliere, Estelle Zoe	October 29, 1882
Dumont, Fermand	February 4, 1901
Dupris, Maximilien	September 18, 1906
Dussart, August	April 25, 1883
Emile, Henri	September 4, 1906
Esgain, Aime	October 1, 1906
Esgain, Octave	October 1, 1906
Favesse, Gustave	May 9, 1891
Flemal, Cornelius	May 27, 1893
Flemal, Pierre	October 5, 1893
Franco, Joseph	August 28, 1897
Frere, Francois	October 16, 1900
Frere, Louis	August 30, 1898
Frere, Louis	September 8, 1897
Geniaux, Nester	April 15, 1893
Gennart, Leon	July 4, 1880
Gennaux, John	December 16, 1891
Gillaume, Arthur	August 28, 1890

Gillot, Aime	August 21, 1893
Goossens, Isidore	September 4, 1893
Goossens, Joseph	October 22, 1883
Goossens, Leon	October 22, 1883
Gouverneur, Ernest	October 2, 1900
Guignard, Gaston	April 24, 1915
Gunaux, Gustux	August 22, 1891
Hancart, August	October 18, 1893
Hans, August	August 3, 1894
Henri, Emile	September 4, 1906
Henri, Palidore	April, 1880
Henry, Frank	November 11, 1892
Houeyaux, Jules	February 14, 1907
Houssiere, Arthur	November 29, 1892
Hulet, Arthur	September 4, 1893
Jacquet, Leon	September 11, 1891
Jacquet, Nicholas	August 27, 1892
Jacquit, Joseph	August 21, 1889
Jasmes, Jean Francois	October 10, 1893
Jaye, Loon	May, 1890
Joris, Vital	October 10, 1890
Joseph, Sortit (?)	December 10, 1890
Kertz, Emile	April 5, 1889
Kinnet, Joseph	September 1, 1892
Lachapel, Arthur	July1, 1892
Lalieu, George Marc	December 29, 1892
Lambillotte, John	September 11, 1891
Lambillotte, Oscar	November 6, 1901
Lammbiotte, Jules	October 6, 1892
Lannoy, Peter	1888
Lardinois, August	April 23, 1892
Laroche, Alphonse	August 23, 1893
Lavergue, Emile	September 4, 1893
Ledoux, Henry	September 5, 1881
Lefebre, Gustave	September 26, 1893
Lefebure, Arthur	November 21, 1906
Lefever, Gustave	September 23, 1893
Lefevre, Alphonse	October 10, 1885
Lefevre, Estelle Zoe	October 29, 1882
Legros, John	November 26, 1881
Lemaigre, Emile	August 23, 1893

27

Lemaire, Alfred	August 21, 1893
Lemaitre, Emile	September 5, 1892
Lemire, Leopold	April 22, 1892
Leroy, Edmond	November 8, 1905
Leroy, John Baptist	November 8, 1905
Loriaux, Antoine	August 24, 1880
Loriaux, Gustave	December 2, 1892
Luyckx, Alfred	October 18, 1893
Mandelier, Jack	August 17, 1893
Mannoyer, Arthur	October 13, 1891
Marchent, Joseph	December 4, 1893
Marlie, Annie	March, 1893
Marlier, Jule	November 11, 1892
Martin, Alaxandre	September 2, 1884
Martin, Rome	July 3, 1891
Mascaux, Joseph	October 1, 1906
Mausy, Theophile	September 10, 1893
Menter, Alexis	August 29, 1893
Michaux, Jean Baptiste	September 4, 1893
Molle, G. B.	February 5, 1895
Molle, Desire	January 15, 1892
Neil, Alfred	September 23, 1893
Neukerman, Octave	October 1, 1906
Nicaise, Frederic	October 8, 1887
Nicholas, Frank	March 12, 1896
Niset, Julus	1890
Palidore, Henri	April, 1880
Pettit, Leon	February, 1882
Pierre, Antoine	August 15, 1889
Pierre, Hubert	September 15, 1892
Pierre, Joseph	November 15, 1889
Pierson, Eugene	January 18, 1893
Pivont, Arile	August 8, 1890
Predt, Camille	August 23, 1893
Quintin, Edmond	October 6, 1900
Raffler, Edmond	August 21, 1907
Ravaux, Isador	October 29, 1903
Roffler, Edmond	August 15, 1873
Roffler, Edmond	August 21, 1907
Rosseaux, Jack	September 1, 1891
Rosseaux, Nicholas	September 2, 1891

Roussaux, John (Jean)	May 16, 1891
Rousseau, John B.	October 1, 1906
Rousseaux, Charles	August 23, 1893
Rousseaux, Jacque	September 1, 1891
Schmidt, Frank	December 20, 1903
Serat, August	November 23, 1893
Soupart, Adolphe	August 21, 1893
Stassin, Leopold	October 10, 1893
Swain, Gustave	September, 1901
Swain, Leon	December 18, 1879
Theophile, Mausy	September 10, 1893
Thirret, Aimable	August 14, 1894
Thirret, Leon	August 14, 1894
Van More, Joseph	April 14, 1888
Van More, Peter	October 14, 1893
Vanderman, Leopold	August 29, 1893
Vandervelde, Charles	September 19, 1893
Velian, John	March, 1888
Wallet, Hector	September 8, 1894
Wallot, Amie	August 3, 1903
Watrin, Edward	October 3, 1892
Weary, Leon	April 8, 1893
Weary, Louis	September 11, 1894
William, Amil	January 18, 1888
Williamne, Gustave	----------
Wulffing, Alexandre	September 10, 1893

FRENCHMEN APPLYING FOR CITIZENSHIP IN BLACKFORD COUNTY

Name	Date of Arrival
Barr, Alcide	October 23, 1891
Barr, Charles	June 14, 1888
Barr, John	September 3, 1892
Bayle, Arsene	March 14, 1892
Brasseur, Emile	October 15, 1890
Caucho, Victor	February 15, 1892
Cotton, Charles	August 1, 1894
Dhe, Charles	October 24, 1892
Deenes, Camille	September 22, 1902
Deleruyelle, Anatole	August 21, 1900

Denis, Camille	September 22, 1902
Dufour, Fredrich	August 22, 1900
Fredman, Andrew	July 6, 1843 (Alsace)
Frere, Emile	December 18, 1895
Grandejean, Joseph	September 28, 1895
Granger, Gilbert	August 10, 1862
Joice, Andre	July 19, 1867
Landauer, Albert	November 4, 1874
Marra, Richard	July 14, 1892
Marshall, Eugene	1889
Masgana, Emmanuel	August 27, 1893
Pettit, Arthur	March, 1882
Tanchon, Auguste	January, 1891
Trauschou, Victor	February 15, 1892

INCIDENTS OF EARLY GAS AND OIL DAYS RECALLED
BY FORMER RESIDENT VISITING HERE

J. M. Reasoner, of Minneapolis, formerly for many years a resident of Hartford City, who is visiting friends here at the present time, recalls some interesting facts about the early gas and oil boom days in Hartford City. He recounted today, for a reporter for the Times Gazette, some of these incidents.

The first discovery of gas in this territory was made in Eaton in 1887. Mr. Carter, of Eaton, was the head of the company owning this well, which was called Carter well. Excursion trains from Fort Wayne and nearby towns started, and this well caused much excitement among the people. The next well known to be drilled was near Montpelier. This was, however, for oil and was drilled by William Schull. Excursions were also sent to Montpelier as well as to Eaton.

The next well was drilled in Hartford City and was a gas well. This was near where the Lake Erie depot now stands on property then owned by Samuel Gadbury. Some time later the large "Jumbo" well close to where Walnut Street crosses the Pennsylvania was shot. It was then on property owned by John Leonard. This was a very large well, and pipes were run from this well all over the city. A great display was made by lighting the ends of the tubes piped from this well, which caused large fires. Hundreds of these lights were going night and day and arches were constructed in different parts of the town and were lighted. The gas was also piped to the country, usually to a crossroad where there would be four different pipes branching off. From thirty to forty farmers would use from these pipes and would keep the back yard and front yard at the homes lighted nights. As far away as Marion the reflection could be seen in the sky. The gas was used to cook, heat and light. The natural gas pressure with 300 pounds to the square inch, but regulators were used.

In 1890 the legislature put forth a bill prohibiting the out door torch lighting. The size of Hartford City at that time was about 2500 population. At that time a well was also drilled in the Southside which went to the city by the purchase of forty acres for the glass factory soon to be built. This well was given as a sort of donation.

This was the establishment of the American Window Glass factory which was then the third largest glass factory in the world. The town grew quickly by the influx of workers. A good bit of this land, which was purchased by the city for the factory, was made out in lots, and houses were built where the employees and their families could live, which would be near the factory. Mr. Cantwell was the first secretary of the factory, and Richard Heagany, well known resident of this city, was the first manager.

THE BULGARIANS

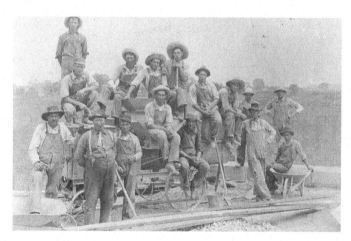

A work crew laying a stone bed for the railroad.

July 1, 1907

BULGARIAN WORKMEN TURN OUT
TO BURY COMPATRIOT

Man Who Dropped Dead While At Work
Interred in Oddfellows Cemetery

Lalo Evanof, the Bulgarian who was found dead Friday along the Ohio Oil Company's pipeline in Washington Township, was buried Sunday at 1 p.m. at Oddfellows' Cemetery. His fellow workmen, about forty in number, walked to this city in the morning, made arrangements to pay the funeral expenses and formed a procession to the cemetery following the hearse. There were no services. The dead man had worked for nearly a month without drawing his wages and the money will be forwarded to his family in his native country. He was 48 years old.

Daily Times Gazette   March 5, 1912

The coal heaver accidentally killed at the Sneath Glass Company about three o'clock Monday afternoon was not an Italian nor was his name William Jim. He was Glizar Dineff, a Bulgarian and he was 18 years of age. The body of the unfortunate man was shipped to Granite City, Illinois, where there is a Bulgarian colony and where a priest of his own nationality will conduct the services. The body was accompanied by his brother Tom Dineff who took a job at the South Side factory Monday after being idle about six months. The brothers came to this city about a year ago to work on the Pennsylvania Railroad construction work. Besides the brother the dead man is survived by parents who live in the native country. The Sneath Glass stood the expense of the burial and transportation to Illinois.

<u>Daily Times Gazette</u>   March 29, 1912

Coroner's finding in the death of Glizar Dineff, crushed to death on March 4 while unloading a car load of coal at the Sneath, had his back broken when he was buried beneath the coal from the car. He had been warned not to stand in the position he was in when he dislodged the coal with a long iron bar. The coroner placed the blame for his death on the man himself.

<u>Daily Times Gazette</u>   October 26, 1912

TWO BULGARIANS RETURN HOME TO JOIN ARMY

With lamentations and many maledictions against King Ferdinand of Bulgaria, two Bulgarians, Nidelch Miteff and Steve Esposinka, employed on the Pennsylvania section gang, answered the bidding of a cablegram from their native land to come back and help fight for their country. Miteff has been in America two years and can speak the language fairly well while the other fellow who has been here a year, does not speak so well. Both were employed at the American Window Glass factory last winter. The command to return and fight was received by them with great sorrow as they are greatly attached to their adopted country, but their loyalty to their native land made them anxious to get back and fight for Bulgaria.

It is a rule in the army there that all Bulgarians shall be a member of the army at the age of 18 and shall be a soldier until he is 38 years old. Both Bulgarians had about a $1000 apiece which they had saved from their labor here. It will take them 38 days to make the trip back home.

<u>Daily Times Gazette</u>   November 26, 1912

ANOTHER BULGARIAN GOES HOME TO FIGHT

"Why don't you come home? Every child who can carry a gun is helping in the war" was the message received a few days ago by James Nedeff, a Bulgarian, employed in the machine room at the South Side factory, from his parents in Bulgaria, who, it is claimed, have not seen him in ten years.

Nedeff left Monday afternoon for New York where he will sail for his native country. It is said that the parents have written him on numerous occasions to come home and see them, but Nedeff never showed much concern until he received the above message.

Nedeff, who was employed as operator of one of the blowing machines, is said by workmen to be one of the most Americanized foreigners that has ever been employed at the factory. He is able to speak the American tongue fluently and has been employed here for the past several years. During his stay here, he always sent his money which he received for his work, back to Bulgaria where he had placed it on deposit. He wrote for his money a few days ago and word came back that he could not get it unless he came after it. His parents had notified the bank officials not to send it to him as they knew he would not come home if he got his money. He claimed he had $3000 in the bank. It is the law in Bulgaria that the advice of the parents shall be taken in all matters and so Nedeff was refused his money. Before leaving Nedeff said to the workmen at the factory that he would be back before long if he did not get killed in the war.

Evening News   August 16, 1914

WAR SEVERS PARTNERSHIP

The European conflict has broken up the first partnership started by the newer element of Hartford City's foreign population, that of the grocery firm of Pete Peshoft and Tony Dineff, whose store is located at the corner of 7th and Jefferson Streets where George Turner formerly conducted a grocery. Pete and Tony are Bulgarians. The partners recently received a call from the Bulgarian government to return to the colors. Although Bulgaria is not yet at war, the two Hartford City grocers are of the age at which men of that country are supposed to enter the army. Unless he returns when the government calls him to war, a Bulgarian does not dare return to his native land at any future time, for he would do so at the risk of his life.

When the call came, Pete Peshoft, 21, elected to return for 3 years service while his partner relinquished his claim on Bulgaria and will remain in peaceful America. He does not ever intend to return to his native country. Pete left here for Indianapolis, where he will go to New York City and then seek passage to Bulgaria.

The new store is enjoying a good business, especially from the foreign population of the South Side. Besides groceries Deniff handles meats. He keeps a clean and inviting looking store.

Several days ago a party of Bulgarians arrived in this city from Canada.

They brought with them a quantity of Canadian paper money, which they seem to have spent freely, for a number of merchants have received the Canadian bills. The money is worth its fair value in this country.

<u>Evening News</u>   March 1, 1915

DO NOT WISH TO RETURN TO HOME

The foreigners in this city are not as eager to return in the defense of their fatherland at this time as they were at the time the Balkan* war broke out, as was shown Saturday afternoon when two young Bulgarians appeared in the office of the county clerk where one of them had a paper made out for the purpose of granting a lawyer living in their home town, the power of attorney in regulating their estates there.

One of the young men, by the name of Steve Donneff, has been in this country for several years and is a very good student of the language. He is able to carry on a good conversation in English. Naturalization papers were taken out by this young man some time ago and at that time, when questioned by the county clerk he said the people in the old country do not know what they are fighting for and that they are in the war because they were told to be.

Young Donneff appeared with a young man who gave the name of Gencho Pentcheff. On account of his previous visits to the office at that time when he took out his papers for naturalization, Donneff was allowed to testify as to his companion's name.

According to the young man who wished to take out the papers, he is afraid that his estate, which must amount to considerable in Bulgaria, is in danger of being taken away from him during his absence. Power of attorney was given to George Stytcheff, in Pentcheff's home town in Bulgaria.

When the foreigners were asked why they did not go to their homes and attend to the business for themselves, they said they did not wish to join the army now.

*In 1912, with Russian encouragement, Bulgaria, Greece, Montenegro, and Serbia formed the Balkan League, which started a war with the Ottoman empire. Increasing tension and discontent among the Slavic peoples resulted in the assassination of Archduke Franz Ferdinand, the heir to the Habsburg throne, in Sarajevo, Bosnia, on June 28, 1914. Balkan national conflicts thus provided the incident that pulled all of Europe into World War I. (Encyclopedia <u>Americana</u>)

Evening News   August 31, 1915

Steven N. Donneff, born in Bulgaria, a glassworker, and Miss Erma Lambiotte, 16, daughter of Jules Lambiotte, were granted a marriage license, and were married in the county clerk's office by Deputy Clerk Lewis Reeves, The bride's mother accompanied them to the office and gave her consent to the marriage.

Evening News   November 22, 1915

"FREEZE OUT" THIRD PARTNER

The crowding out of one of the three Bulgarian proprietors of a Southside bakery by the other two has led to the filing of two suits in the circuit court, one for partition of real estate and the other for the appointment of a receiver and sale of the bakery.

Tasko Belcheff, through his attorneys, Waltz & Emshwiller, has brought both suits against Mitre Petroff and Gasho Dineff. Belcheff asks a commissioner be appointed for the partition of lot number four, in the Cantwell and Patterson addition.

In his other complaint, against the same parties, Tasko sets out that the partnership was formed on December 19, 1914, and in the month of November, this year, the other two partners have taken full possession of the bakery, refusing to allow the plaintiff about the premises, to clerk in the store or to get his portion of the profits. Tasko declares that Mitre and Gasho have misapplied funds belonging to the partnership to their own use and have failed to make an accounting with him and have refused to allow him to know anything about the condition of the business or anything about where the money is going. The plaintiff declares he does not, for these reasons, know in what amount the other two partners are indebted to him.

Belcheff sets out that the firm has a valuable stock and considerable valuable machinery and a good trade. He asks that a receiver be appointed to sell the business and divide, after all debts are settled, the money equally among the three.

Evening News   February 17, 1916

CLAIMS HE IS SERB SOLDIER

A Servian (sic) giving his name as Satir Anstasoff has arrived in Hartford City and is now looking for work in one of the factories here. He states that he recently served in the Servian (sic) army in the operations against Austria.

Anstasoff claims that he was wounded three times while in the service and that at the present time he is in a serious condition. According to Southside residents who saw him he has the wounds to prove that he has recently been in battle.

The foreigner states that he was on the Atlantic forty-five days, on his trip to America. He has never been to the United States before, he has told countrymen here, and cannot speak English. Other Servians (sic) on the Southside have talked with him and to them he has told his story.

Anstoff states that he arrived in New York City last Saturday. He relates terrible battle scenes, according to those who have talked with him and seems to have had all the war he wants.

Daily Times Gazette   March 14, 1919

FORMER RESIDENT DIED FROM FLU

Tony Deniff, formerly proprietor of a grocery store on the corner of 7th and Jefferson Streets, died at Hammond, Indiana, after an illness with influenza. He left here about a year ago for Hammond where he set up in the grocery business. His funeral was held March 2nd according to word received here.

BULGARIANS APPLYING FOR CITIZENSHIP IN BLACKFORD COUNTY

Name	Date of Arrival
Belcheff, Tasco	March 7, 1915 (Serbia)
Dimoff, George	July 5, 1912 (Serbia)
Doneff, Steve	April 29, 1901
Pentcheff, Gentcho	April 4, 1914
Swanoff, Nikolia	April 4, 1914
Todoroff, Trifon	April 4, 1914
Urdonoff, Kris	May 1, 1914

THE CANADIANS

PETER JOHN LONEY

Peter John Loney was born in Cornwall, Ontario, Canada on January 29, 1847. He married Mary Catherine Dickinson, who was born in Scotland and at the age of two weeks, came with her family to Canada.

In 1890 the couple came to Hartford City from Ft. Wayne, Indiana, where Mr. Loney, an architect, served in that capacity for the rebuilding of the Hartford City Paper Mill which had been destroyed by fire. After the rebuilding had been completed the couple continued to reside here. Mr. Loney then engaged in his own business enterprise. He was the architect for many of the fine Hartford City homes built at that time.

P. J. and Mary Loney were parents of three children: Lawrence (born October 17, 1880), Mrs. Emma Corcoran of Lima, Ohio, and Tom McMahon of White Bear, Minnesota. Peter John also had a brother Allen Loney from Ontario, Canada.

Evening News   May 25, 1894

P. J. Loney, the architect, has prepared the plans for a residence to be erected by W. R. Krauss on North High Street (now Keplinger Funeral Home). It is to be a modern two-story frame and will cost $3000. The first floor will contain six rooms; the upper story five bedrooms and a bathroom. Altogether it will be one of the most elegant residences in the city. Work will begin on it next week and it will be rushed to completion as rapidly as possible.

Telegram   September 26, 1894

Architect P. J. Loney is back from Winipeg. His visit was cut short by an eager and a nipping air which is an adjunct of the climate of Manitoba at this time. The time for an inhabitant of the temperate zone to visit Winipeg is in the glad summer time.

Telegram   May 29, 1895

Architect Loney is preparing plans for a brick building for the Telegram. It will be erected on the lot on Jefferson Street, half a square north of the court house, recently purchased by the Telegram. The building will be arranged especially for the newspaper business and will be convenient of access to the business public.

    May, 1898 Bids for building the J. Dowell house (Blackford County Historical Society located at 321 North High Street) will be received by Architect Loney.

Telegram   March 30, 1899

Architect Loney last night returned from Martinsville where he has been spending a few weeks for his health. While there Mr. Loney secured considerable architectural work which includes plans for two handsome residences and a business block.

Evening News   April 13, 1899

J. U. Dick block to be rebuilt—Architect P. J. Loney

Evening News   November 6, 1900

P. J. Loney, the architect, came from Ft. Wayne last night to vote. Mr. Loney is now connected with the office of one of the leading architects of Ft. Wayne. P. J. has moved his family to Ft. Wayne.

Evening News   December 22, 1914

FORMER HARTFORD CITY BOY WINS
FAME AS RAILROAD ARCHITECT

Although it has been several years since he left here, there are still many who will remember Thomas McMahon, stepson of P. J. Loney, the architect, and a half brother of Lawrence Loney of this city. These will be interested to know that Tom has made a success of life and is now the general architect of the Great Northern Railroad, a very responsible position for a young man. Tom was at one time a delivery boy for a local grocery firm. He came here with his stepfather and his work in architecture was as a tracer in his father's office when the first plant of the Ft. Wayne Corrugated Paper Mill was erected. When he left here, he took employment with F. A. Bartlett, general architect of the C. B. & Q. in Chicago. Bartlett afterward went to the Great Northern at St. Paul, and he took Tom with him. Bartlett resigned some time ago and Tom succeeded him. President Hill at once put him to work on the construction work in Glacier Park, the pet project of Hill. McMahon designed most of the buildings there and has won fame as an architect.

CANADIANS APPLYING FOR CITIZENSHIP IN BLACKFORD COUNTY

Name	Date of Arrival
Baines, Fred	September 22, 1897
Ballam, Sydney	January 2, 1894
Brindamore, Arthur	November 3, 1888
Earnest, William	May 10, 1848
Gannom, Leon	October 7, 1887
Gannon, Lewis	May 1, 1876
Gannon, Napoleon	October, 1861
Irwin, William	May 20, 1866
Johnson, Thomas	October 15, 1883
Loney, Lawrence	1885
Marsland, Edward	October 5, 1898
McClintic, Allan	September, 1902
McClintick, John	September, 1901
McDonell, Frederick	October 14, 1891
McGuiness, Thomas	January 9, 1861
Murphey, William	April 15, 1859
Quinn, John	October 6, 1863
Scott, David	June 28, 1904
Scott, George	August 4, 1897
Scott, John	April 28, 1902
Stroner, Robert	1881
Young, Will	February, 1899

THE CHINESE

We Lead, Others Follow_____

Shirts, Collars and Cuffs
Our Specialty.

New Method Laundry

'PHONE 255 - 223 WEST WASHINGTON STREET
Hartford City, Indiana

Sam Lee was still involved with the "New Method Laundry" as his advertisement shows in the 1899 City Directory.

SAM LEE, CHINESE

With little information to go on, we know that in 1893 Hartford City had a Chinese laundry man by the name of Sam Lee. References to him in the newspaper are as follows:

<u>Hartford City Telegram</u>   May 11, 1893

The almond eyed celestial who was in town last week lays claim to the name of Sam Hong, instead of Wun Lung as this paper stated last week. He is Americanized, but still wears a cue (sic), that he may some day return to his own country without shame and mortification. Hong is not the man from Hong Kong in song; he is simply a laundry man. He is educated and writes a good hand. He comes here from Union City to take charge of the laundry belonging to S. B. Patterson.

<u>Telegram</u>   April 24, 1895

Sam Lee, the celestial child of the Orient who mangles dirty linen at his laundry on West Washington Street, was last night cruelly victimized by rude American thieves who stole from him $5 and a "lazor' what you shave whiskers with."

<u>Evening News</u>   June 6, 1898

The Chinese Boy

Lum Sam's Nephew Visits Him and is Introduced to the Wash Tub Straightway

The Chinese population in this town is increasing. Lum Sam is prospering to such an extent that he had to send for his nephew, who arrived yesterday. The greeting Lum gave the newcomer, who is a youth probably seventeen years old, was unique. Sam did not even shake hands with him. When the boy, who for convenience might just as well be called Swi Lung as anything else, arrived at Lum Sam's laundry, Sam marched him right back and introduced him to the wash tub. There was no ceremony nor exchange of courtesies, no questioning after the health of Swi or his relatives. It was business from the word "go." Sam was behind with his work; he had recently been squeezed by the authorities on the flagitious charge of provoke and he was working his fingers off to catch up with himself. For these reasons it is supposed that Sam dispensed with the usual celestial greeting.

<u>Hartford City Daily Gazette,</u>   June 12, 1903

Chinaman Submits To Haircut

Fink Star, the new Chink who has succeeded to the hand laundry on West Washington Street, is probably the first Chinaman in Hartford City to ever have his hair cut by a barber.

In fact he is the only one who has ever been here who defied the superstition of his country in parting with his pig tail. The impression has prevailed for many years that the natives of that country who sport hair cuts in this country renounce their allegiance to China and are disgraced. Fink is American born and he doesn't care a snap what his countrymen think about his hair cuts, and he climbs into a barber's chair the same as any other person who needs his locks trimmed. Fink came here from Bluffton, where he says it is the style to wong hair and part it in the middle. Fink is eighteen years old.

Daily Times Gazette   September 16, 1908

Sam Lee, the laundryman, has taken the first steps toward becoming an American. He has had his que (sic) cut off and now wears his hair American style. He was careful, however, to save the long braid and if he ever returns to China, it is suspected that Sam will attach the severed que (sic) as a switch.

Daily Times Gazette   October 6, 1908

CHINESE LAUNDRYMAN QUITS

Sam Lee, who has been conducting a laundry in Elton block, quit business—left town, going to Marion. Sam left what little laundry work he had with Dave Kesler and shook the dust of Hartford City from his feet. He took his que (sic) along in his satchel.

Daily Gazette   Advertisement April 4, 1902

L. Q. Lee
Chinese Laundry—West Washington Street
Do All Work Myself
No Girls Employed
Bring Me Your Work
Satisfaction Guaranteed

*correct spelling of the Chinese pigtail is queue

THE COLORED

Blackford County Gazette.

VOL. IX. NO. 29.   HARTFORD CITY, INDIANA, SATURDAY, MAY 28, 1904   NEW SERIES VOL. III,

TWICE MARRIED IN SLAVERY

HENRY HENDERSON, COLORED, HAS INTERESTING LIFE HISTORY

SOLD ON BLOCK AT THE AGE OF 4

Master Took Oath Never to Sell Him And Worry Caused Him to Take His Own Life

Sold on the block in slavery in the streets of Richmond, Virginia, driven in a herd of slaves like as many cattle and once traded for a mule is the early history of Henry Henderson, the oldest colored man in this county and a familiar object of the streets of this city.

Henderson does not know his own age, but thinks he is over 78. He was four years old when torn from the side of his parents and driven away and never saw them afterwards. He and a little girl, a few years his senior, were sold together and purchased by a wealthy bachelor and taken to Columbia, South Carolina. The elderly man told the slave auctioneer that he had bought the children to raise, that they might attend him in his old age and they would never be sold.

HENRY HENDERSON

One day a wealthy Kentuckian, who was driving his stock to market, stopped over night with the rich old bachelor and took a fancy to the little colored boy and girl. He asked the price of the children but found that they were not for sale. He insisted and pleaded until the old man said he would only consider a trade on one condition, and that was that the Kentuckian, whose name was Samuel Reicher would take a solemn oath that he would never sell the children or separate them. Reicher made the oath and for their payment left a mule, which at that time was on a par

with a negro slave. The children were driven across the country to Kentucky to a small gig to the farm of Charles Reicher, the father of Samuel Reicher.

When young, Reicher reached home he found that Lawrence Lamont, his partner, had left the country and taken with him all the proceeds of the sale of the stock and left only the debts for Reicher. The sheriff came with an execution to seize his property. Reicher was greatly worried for fear that the children would be levied on by the sheriff. It preyed upon his mind until he came deranged and he sent a bullet into his brain.

His father, Charles Reicher, paid off the indebtedness and kept the oath taken by the son, never to sell nor separate the little colored boy and girl. Twice married in slavery, the old negro remained with his master until the end of the war, when he went to work for himself. He soon earned himself a farm and lived there and raised a family.

About four years ago he came north to Indianapolis where he lived two years with his daughter, Mrs. George Green, in that city. At that time they moved here and this has been his home ever since. He is a familiar object on the streets and the only colored residents here who salutes the white men with a bow and tip of the hat. One of his greatest boasts is that he was "a good nigger" and never received a lick after he grew to be a man. He is happy and contented.

Henry Henderson had once been a slave. He lived in Blackford County with his daughter.

Cyrus "Pony" Williams chatting with some local citizens in Montpelier, Indiana.

George D. Stevens, 1859-1940

George Stevens lived in Hartford City, Indiana, for approximately 30 years with no one knowing he was "black." He was a prominent official at the Fort Wayne Corrugated Paper Mill.

African Americans

Several black Americans have lived in Blackford County, some for only a short time, some for many years. They were very likeable, hard working citizens. These are the stories of a few of them.

<u>Daily Gazette</u>   July 7, 1902

Hartford City's colored population is showing a rapid increase. For years the colored population in the entire county did not exceed ten and the number of families not more than three. Within the past year it has grown in Hartford City alone to at least fifty in total numbers. The National Rolling Mill probably employs more colored laborers than any other concern in the city. They are used to load and unload the cars at the mill. The remainder of the population find employment at various locations. The greatest number, aside from the rolling mill, are doing porter work.

One thing can be said of the colored residents of Hartford City, they are industrious and law-abiding. No colored person has been in police court for eight or ten years. Baden, the colored man from Montpelier who shot Granville Shepp in a saloon at the oil town, is the first colored man to receive a sentence in the circuit court for at least twenty years.

<u>Daily Gazette</u>   June 10, 1903

POOR FARM ASYLUM FOR PONY WILLIAMS

Pony Williams, the first colored man ever allowed to take up abode in Montpelier came down to Hartford City to make application to the trustee for admission to the County poor farm.

Williams is not an old man but has met with misfortune and is unable to work any longer. The past few years he has been acting in the capacity of porter at Jackson's saloon. He met with a misfortune some time ago and has been unable to work since. His right hand and arm are swollen to twice their normal size and give him much pain. He says it was caused from a sprain, but the man who accompanied him here said that it was caused by a snake bite and that blood poisoning had set in. Gola Patton, the trustee was out of the city all day and Pony was compelled to wait until late in the evening. He is thought a great deal of by Montpelier people and has many friends there, who were surprised when they learned of his intention.

July 28, 1903

Pony Williams the first colored man ever allowed to stay in Montpelier and who has been at the county farm, went back to the Oil city Monday. Pony was laid up for some time with blood poisoning in his arm and on account of his inability to work was taken to the county infirmary. He is getting along nicely and has gone back to work as he is too proud to board off the county when he is able to do for himself.

<u>Blackford County Gazette</u>   May 28, 1904

TWICE MARRIED IN SLAVERY

Sold on the block in slavery in the street of Richmond, Virginia, driven in a herd of slaves like as many cattle and once traded for a mule is the early history of Henry Henderson, the oldest colored man in this county and a familiar object on the streets of this city.

Henderson does not know his own age, but thinks he is over 78. He was four years old when torn from the side of his parents and driven away and never saw them afterwards. He and a little girl, a few years his senior, were sold together and purchased by a wealthy bachelor and taken to Columbia, South Carolina. The elderly man told the slave auctioneer that he had bought the children to raise, that they might attend him in his old age and they would never be sold.

One day a wealthy Kentuckian, who was driving his stock to market, stopped over night with the rich old bachelor and took a fancy to the little colored boy and girl. He asked the price of the children but found that they were not for sale. He insisted and pleaded until the old man said he would only consider a trade on one condition, and that was that the Kentuckian, whose name was Samuel Reicher, would take a solemn oath that he would never sell the children or separate them. Reicher made the oath and for their payment left a mule, which at the time was on a par with a negro slave. The children were driven across the country to Kentucky in a small rig to the farm of Charles Reicher, the father of Samuel Reicher.

When young Reicher reached home he found that Lawrence Lamont, his partner, had left the country and taken with him all the proceeds of the sale of the stock and left only the debts for Reicher. The sheriff came with an execution to seize his property. Reicher was greatly worried for fear that the children would be levied only by the sheriff. It preyed upon his mind until he became deranged and he sent a bullet into his brain.

His father, Charles Reicher, paid off the indebtedness and kept the oath taken by the son, never to sell nor separate the little colored boy and girl. Twice married in slavery, the old negro remained with his master until the end of the war, when he went to work for himself. He soon earned himself a farm and lived there and raised a family.

About four years ago he came north to Indianapolis where he lived two years with his daughter, Mrs. George Green, in that city. At that time they moved here and this has been his home every since. He is a familiar object on the streets and the only colored resident here who salutes the white man with a bow and tip of the hat. One of his grandest boasts is that he was "a good nigger" and never received a lick after he grew to be a man. He is happy and contented.

Daily Times Gazette   September 11, 1906

MARIETTA WANTED TO COMMIT MURDER

Marietta Summers, the Montpelier colored woman who is in jail here, has been adjudged of unsound mind as the result of an inquest held over her before she was brought here and locked up.

From the Montpelier Herald:

Marietta has been acting strangely for some time and it was not long ago that an account was given in the Herald of her suddenly going away without telling her parents and it was later learned that she had gone to Chicago and was making her home with relatives.

Mrs. Wayne thought it was best that her daughter should receive proper attention and so she filed the affidavit for the inquest. It was held at the Mayor's office before John Boyd, Mayor Schneider and Doctors Sellers, Thornton and Emshwiller and they were not long in declaring her insane.

Although her talk was not of a rational order, she said that she had a great desire to kill someone and when asked how she intended to do it, she said by strangling them. She also said she seriously intended to set some building on fire. She was taken to Hartford City yesterday by William Reynolds where she will remain until the proper papers can be made out and arrangements can be made to have her lodged in East Haven. (The insane asylum at Richmond, Indiana)

Yesterday the prisoner tore up her bed clothing and took all the feathers out of the pillows and threw them out the windows. Marietta will probably have a good time there in Hartford City this week while the carnival is going on as her cell window overlooks the street where the festival is to be given.

Evening News   December 17, 1906

Saturday night in the rooms of the bride's son-in-law and daughter in the Dowell block on the south side of the square took place the marriage of John R. Fowler and Mrs. Louise Burden, a colored couple who came here from Chicago to have the matrimonial knot tied. Reverend Louis Reeves performed the ceremony. Both have been married before, each having been divorced.

In securing a license the bride gave her home as Hartford City and so did the bridegroom. She is 36 and her husband is 28 years old. The bride has two children.

Daily Times Gazette   March 18, 1912

Considerable space was devoted to children born on February 29, but the stork took matters in hand and celebrated St. Patrick's Day by bringing a little son to Mr. and Mrs. Arthur Shaffer, well known colored residents.

Daily Times Gazette   April 26, 1912

RED HEAD IN CAPTIVITY

What is believed to be the only redheaded colored person in captivity occupies a cell at the Montpelier lockup. The peculiar specimen is George Grimsley, who until several months ago was employed as a porter in local barber shops. Grimsley gave a dance at his home Thursday night and partook of the liquid refreshments too liberally. He was fined $5 and costs by Mayor Burris and given his choice of paying or staying. He stayed.

Evening News   October 9, 1915

COLORED COUPLE MARRIED

John H. Robinson and May Anthony were married by Squire Lucas at his office last evening. The groom is a swell coon who lives at Marion and the bride is a colored young lady who has been employed as a domestic in this city.

Mr. and Mrs. Robinson departed for Marion this morning, and their unmistakable happiness attracted attention at the Panhandle station. Robinson was still attired in his swallow-tail coat and his spring overcoat could not hide the clawhammer. The couple paced the platform and became so absorbed in each other that they involuntarily engaged in a cake walk to the music of the love that sang in their hearts.

The spectators did not know Mr. and Mrs. Robinson, but they could not repress a silent wish for their future happiness.

Daily Times Gazette   May 8, 1920

STEVE GARRISON IN STATE DELEGATION

The Indiana delegation to the presidential nominating convention of the Socialist party, to be held in New York, is made up of the following: Edward Henry, Indianapolis; Ross Brown, Muncie; John Lewis, Elwood; Madge P. Stevens, Terre Haute; A. J. Hart, Richmond; S. C. Garrison, Montpelier.

Mr. and Mrs. Garrison came to Montpelier in the late 1800's and lived on West Huntington Street. Mr. Garrison was a plasterer and then became the janitor at the Farmers Deposit Bank. He was highly regarded as a scholar and philosopher and was well educated. Politically he followed the doctrines of Eugene V. Debs, the national head of the Socialist party. (Montpelier Yesterday Today Tomorrow p. 31)

Daily Times Gazette   December 2, 1924

FORMER LOCAL BARBER CALLED

Word has been received here of the death of Arthur Smith, 48, of Marion, formerly a colored barber of this city, a son of Al Smith, who conducted a barber shop in South Jefferson Street. Mr. Smith died Sunday evening following a three weeks' illness with uremic poisoning.

Hartford City News   November 30, 1925

"PONY" WILLIAMS, NEGRO, DIES AT MONTPELIER

Cyrus "Pony" Williams, 50, colored, died Sunday morning at 7 o'clock at Montpelier, after a brief illness with acute indigestion.

Mr. Williams was the first negro to ever reside in Montpelier. He has resided there for the past 30 years. Funeral services will be conducted at 3:30 Tuesday afternoon with burial at Montpelier. One sister, Catherine Brodgers, of Chicago, survives. Mr. Williams was employed as the janitor at the hotel.

1986 Blackford County History

GEORGE STEVENS' SECRET

Hartford City had the shock of its existence in April, 1940. It was shortly after the April 8th death of George D. Stevens, 81, in the Blackford County Hospital that local residents learned that Mr. Stevens was "black" rather than "white."

Mr. Stevens was a prominent official at the Fort Wayne Corrugated Paper Mill and widely known Hartford City philanthropist. He lived in one room in the Hotel Hartford for 30 years with his secret, masquerading as a white man.

The record of his death from the Blackford County Health Department, signed by a doctor, stated that George D. Stevens was 81, "white and widowed." Primary cause of his death was Chronic Myocarditis.

Brief funeral services were conducted for this distinguished gentleman at the Burk and Fennig Funeral Home by Reverend H. W. Fox, pastor of the Grace Methodist Church. Commitment services and burial were held in Akron, Ohio, Stevens' birthplace. It was here that local friends and business associates discovered that Stevens was "black" and that all of his relatives there were black.

Unquestionably, this distinguished and highly respected man's secret was like a bombshell explosion, catching the entire community off guard and with absolutely no one admitting, "I knew it all the time."

A 1958 issue of *Ebony* magazine stated, "Stevens came to Hartford City in 1911. He was one of the city's wealthiest men. When he died, the paper mill shut down for half a day; the local paper ran a long story on its front page, followed by a glowing editorial. Some of the top citizens drove to Akron, Ohio, less than 300 miles away, where George had directed that he be buried…"

Stevens was distinguished appearing, slightly built and sporting a Van-Dyke beard. He was chauffeured every day to and from his work at the paper mill. George never approached anyone; he would sit in the lobby of the hotel and if anyone wanted to speak to him, they would have to come to him.

The Ebony story indicated that Stevens crossed the color line after the tragic death of his wife prior to coming to Hartford City. An Akron prominent businessman and boyhood pal of Stevens stated, "Nobody can judge George. He judged himself and being a severe man he sentenced himself to a life of loneliness. This was the only way George could achieve the great things he did for Hartford City. I admire him keeping his secret and I'm proud he was my friend."

THE GERMANS

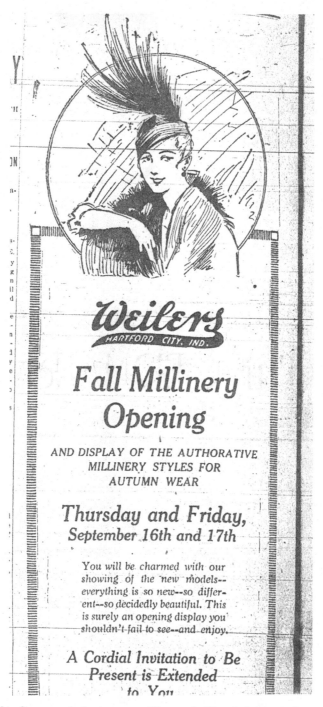

Weilers Store was in business over 50 years in Hartford City and provided a large selection of high quality merchandise for local citizens.

KIRSHBAUM, WINTERS & CO.,

Headquarters for

DRY GOODS,

Clothing,

BOOTS, SHOES, CARPETS, &C.

:o:

MILLINERY a Specialty.

:o:

Hartford City, Ind.

:o:

KIRSHBAUM, WINTERS & Co , beg to inform the Ladies of Hartford City and throughout the County, that they have the Agency for

E. BUTTERICK & CO'S

CELEBRATED

Patterns of Garments

—FOR—

LADIES, MISSES AND CHILDREN.

:o:

Gentlemen's and Boys' Shirt Patterns a Specialty.

:o:

☞ Every Lady who procures a Pattern, receives with it the most minute instructions regarding material, form, and manner of putting the garment together. Provided she follows these instructions, she can cut, make and trim, with the most perfect ease, any gar~~~~ ~~he utility and economy of the process are so apparent, that these Pattern~ ~~~ges, ~~gnized by every lady in the country as a necessity.
☞ 8 sizes sortment of Patterns constantly on hand, and sent to any address, on receipt size and price.

:o:

SUBSCRIPTIONS RECEIVED FOR

RICK & CO'S FASHION PUBLICATIONS.

Sample Copies always on hand.

*Kirshbaum, Winters & Company store advertisement
for 1st rate goods offered in the city.*

Again we call the attention of the citizens of this and adjoining counties to our immense stock of

DRY GOODS,

CLOTHING, HATS, CAPS, BOOTS & SHOES, CARPETS, MILLINERY GOODS,

Groceries and Queensware-

It is generally conceded that our stock is unequalled as to

QUALITY, VARIETY & EXTENT,

and in addition to being

HEADQUARTERS

for all goods in our line, we endeavor to make it to the interest of our customers to buy of us permanently, by giving them goods at the very lowest prices, consistent with good quality and honest quantity. Our policy of always buying our goods direct from first hands has resulted in building up the largest business of the kind in this part of the State, and we are thus enabled to reduce our margin of profits and give our patrons goods at prices far below those of other houses, who pay several intermediate profits.

We thank our patrons for the

LIBERAL PATRONAGE

they have given us in the past, and ask a continuance so long as low prices and fair dealing merit it.

KIRSHBAUM & MAY,

HARTFORD CITY, INDIANA.

David May, founder of L. S. Ayres stores, got his start in the mercantile business in Blackford County as indicated by this 1878 advertisement. Mr. May bought into the Kirshbaum business.

s and Misses' Ready-to-Wear Garmen

Dresses, Waists, Skirts, Furs, etc., ALL THIS SEASON'S STYLES—NOW AT 10%, 25% and 50% L

TS—We Have Arranged Our Coats Into Separate Lots and Have Priced Them Very Low—THE COATS

Lot 3	Lot 4	Lot 5	Lot 6	Lot 7	Lot 8	Lot 9	Lot 10	Lot
:.00. Values up to $12.50, erge, made of l'rsl lamb, ucle, cheviot, bowie, cue big durey, chinchilla and Sale storm serge, now priced at	Values up to $16.50, including novelty and fine fur trim med models, priced now at	Values up to $15.00, wool plushes, velours and large cape cul lars, priced now af	Values up to $20.00, novelty mixtures and novelty cloths, chin chin f'roy cr trimmed, priced	Values up to $22.50, including all the new fabrics, trim med with fur, plush and chaee heav, special now	Values up to $15.00, coats of mellon cloth, lined through out, stout sizes only, priced for this big sale at	Values up to $30.00, plushes, broadcloth, velours and pol morle, some with large fur collars, priced now at	Values up to $15.00, made of melton and zibeline, black only (not this sea on's styles) priced for this sale at	Values up fur or cha or trimming for this big only
$6.48	**$9.98**	**$10.98**	**$12.98**	**$14.48**	**$8.48**	**$18.98**	**$4.98**	**$21.**

A December 1916 Weilers advertisement for women's clothing.

Fred Schuller, a German immigrant from Austria–Hungary, standing in
front of Loney's News Stand. He came in 1913 to avoid World War I.

THE EARLY GERMANS

"Yes, we will go to America. William says it is a fine place to live. Yes, we will go."

Thus might Conrad Cale have addressed his family, holding a letter from his older brother William, his hand trembling slightly. It had been eighteen years since the two brothers had seen each other. William, his pregnant wife Eva, his little son and daughter left their home in Ober-Ramstat, Germany in 1832 to venture across the Atlantic into the unknown wilds of America. Eva's brother, Peter Wedel and his wife Catherine, traveled with them. They lived in the East for few years until in 1838 they settled in east-central Indiana in the as yet unorganized area which would become Blackford County in 1839.

Blackford County was heavily forested, wet and marshy in places, but fertile when cleared and drainage installed. William was a hard worker, a man of vigor, good health and determination, all qualities necessary to the success of the pioneer. Though his future prosperity was probably not counted in a great number of dollars, yet he was satisfied, and frequently urged his brother Conrad to seek his fortune in America and Indiana, also.

It is not easy to uproot oneself and family from familiar surroundings, especially since Conrad was now fifty years old. The difficult decision was made, though it also meant saying goodbye to Susanna, the oldest daughter who was married.

November 15, 1850, Conrad, his wife Elizabeth, his son Jacob and his six daughters arrived in New York. They stopped over in Cincinnati for a short time, and finally arrived at their destination in Blackford County.

William and Conrad Cale's farms were two and three miles north and north-east of the little village of Hartford, in the southeast part of Washington township and the southwest part of Harrison township. The Germans tended to settle close to each other for physical as well as moral support, in times of sickness and death, in times of rejoicing and celebration, in good times and bad.

Peter Hiser and his wife Elizabeth Cale acted as the bank for the German community and often loaned money to family and relatives. In those early days the Germans remained aloof and did not mix with their neighbors.

Nearly all the Germans in the County were devout Lutherans as their ancestors had been for many generations. In the 1840's and 1850's, an itinerant preacher occasionally visited, the worship service sometimes taking place out-of-doors in the shade of tall trees, in the school house, in the court house for very special occasions. In 1866 Zion Lutheran Church was formally organized with six Cales and numerous relatives among the fifty eight signers of the first Constitution.

Conrad Cale died in 1861 and William died in 1879. Each of the wives preceeded her husband in death by a few years. They and some of their children are buried at the Goghnauer Cemetery, northeast of Hartford City. Some other names found on the gravestones are Schwartzkopf, Kleefisch, Schmidt, Willman, Emshwiller and Hiser. The graveyard is now maintained by the township trustee.

It could be said that German was Indiana's second language until the first World War. State laws were published in German as well as English; street signs in some cities were printed in both languages. Many schools taught German as long as a sufficient number of parents desired it. Some small villages were almost perfect replicas of the village from which the inhabitants came from in Germany.

Families tended to retain the language and customs of the homeland in their churches, schools and businesses. The prevalence for doing this was due to two factors. First, Germans outnumbered all other immigrants who came to Indiana. The peak period for German immigration was about 1845 to 1860. Some worked at building railroads and canals, others were skilled in arts and crafts. They were experienced farmers, shrewd and prosperous business and professional men.

The second factor for retaining the language and customs was the Germans' intense love of the fatherland; they did not particularly want to become Americans. Many of these early immigrants planned to return to Germany after amassing enough money to live on comfortably there. Only a small percentage ever returned.

Germans were generally Catholics or Lutherans. Their worship

74

services were conducted in the native tongue until near the end of the 19th century when second, third, and fourth generations opted to become more Americanized. When Germany's belligerence and attacks on neighboring countries led to widespread warfare after 1914, and it seemed likely that the United States would be drawn into the struggle, Germans in America abruptly ceased German church services, teaching German in schools and even conversational German in the home and business. They no longer felt such strong loyalty to the fatherland.

Eventually the German population lost much of its identity, a process hastened by World War I, but of all the foreign peoples that came to this land, Germans held out the longest.

Odds & Ends, Book 1, pages 338-339 Story of David May

Something about the eager youth's persistence and friendly smile impressed a store owner named Kirshbaum.

"If you ever want a job, son, come and see me," he told the young salesman as he bought one of his lithographs.

When the presidential election ended his career as a lithograph salesman, the youth reminded Kirshbaum of his offer. The job, it developed, was that of a clothing salesman in a small store owned by Kirshbaum at Hartford, Indiana, and it paid $25 a month, plus board, room, and washing. The hours were from 6 o'clock in the morning until the store was swept out after closing time, which was sometimes as late as 11 o'clock at night. Young David slept in the rear of the store.

Kirschbaum made him promise to keep the job for at least two years. At the end of this period David's efforts had increased annual sales from $20,000 to $100,000, and on the basis of this record he asked the store manager, named Weiler, for a wage increase.

"Don't be crazy, kid," Weiler told him. "You go back to Cincinnati and instead of asking Kirshbaum for a raise, you tell him you want an interest in the business."

The proposal fairly took away the breath of 20 year-old David, but mustering all his courage, he journeyed to Cincinnati and, pretending a boldness he did not feel, asked Kirshbaum for an interest in the Hartford store. To his astonishment the owner agreed without argument to give him a one-quarter interest, and patted him on the shoulder.

"You get, son, because you've earned it. Now go back and show me how much better you can do."

Promptly David wrote home to his parents about his good fortune, for this rapid advancement never could have come to him in the old country.

For nine years he remained with the Hartford store as part owner. The store was located at the southeast corner of High Street and Washington Street. It was during those years that he began to dream those provoking, stimulating dreams of becoming a merchant prince.

On a bitterly cold night in 1877 a blaze broke out in the building. In frantic haste David set about carrying the clothing stock to a place of safety. Through the night he struggled, first in the scorching heat of the flames, then in the cold wind as he carried the clothing across the street to the courthouse lawn.

He saved the stock but broke his health. He came down with pneumonia, which left him with a hacking cough, and the doctor told him his only hope of avoiding tuberculosis was to move to the dry climate of Colorado. The doctor's ultimatum was a stunning blow, upsetting all his carefully-laid plans. At the time, Colorado was to him merely a part of the Great American Desert.

He sold his interest in the store for $25,000—quite a fortune for an immigrant youth only a few years from the old country—and journeyed to the health resort of Manitou Springs, Colorado, fully intending to return to the East after spending the summer at the health resort.

The Mirror   May 9, 1912

DAVID MAY

Mr. David May. of the Famous and Barr Dry Goods Company, was the epitome of the department store idea. He began his career in a country general store, at Hartford City, Indiana, where every variety of merchandise was carried under one roof—bolts of calico and muslin at one side and barrels of sugar and molasses at the other, with buttons in the show case and tobacco on the shelf. He was the director of a string of enormous mercantile houses which expressed the possibilities of evolution of the primitive department store.

Born at Kaiserslautern, in western Bavaria, of thrifty Jewish parents, he embraced an opportunity to come to America when he was but fourteen years old. He had a cousin in Philadelphia, and a family from Rhine-Palatinate was coming to New York, so the boy took his future in his hand and came along. Finding no immediate opening in Philadelphia, he went to Cincinnati where he learned of a good opening for an energetic clerk in Hartford City. Before he left the store, he had transformed it from a hodge-podge to a carefully systematized establishment. He had already perceived what might be done with department idea.

A troublesome asthmatic affliction sent him to Leadville, Colorado, where he went into business with the Brothers Shoenberg, and when Miss Rosa Shoenberg went to Colorado the summer of 1879, on a visit to the family of her elder brother, the partnership between May and Shoenberg was further cemented by a union of the two houses. Miss Shoenberg became Mrs. David May in 1880. There were four children, Morton, Thomas, Wilbur, and Florence.

From Leadville, Mr. May went to Denver where he further enlarged the department store. In 1903 he came to St. Louis to join with his brothers-in-law in the establishing of the May Company, afterwards consolidated with the Famous. He has a beautiful home in Washington Terrace, and in spite of enormous financial activity, is a devoted family man, a friend to the poor, and a valuable citizen.

<u>Telegram</u>   February 22, 1894

HE BEGAN IN HARTFORD CITY

Mr. J. M. Gardy, the advertising man of "The May" shoe and clothing company, of Denver, says that his firm spends $30,000 a year for advertising in the State papers. The principal proprietor of the "The May" shoe and clothing company is David May, familiarly known all over this section as "Dave." Some years ago "Dave" was part owner of the store now operated by the Weilers. In fact, he began his business career here about twenty-five years ago, and he was then an advertiser whose flaring proclamations from time to time made people open their eyes. He was the first business man in Hartford City to run full-page advertisements of such extent being indeed infrequent at that time anywhere in this section of the country.

"Dave" May left Hartford City, and located in Leadville, Colorado in the days of the craze over its silver developments. He opened a dry goods store there, and his advertising instincts soon made him the best known merchant in all the surrounding camps. He was the leader. Leadville becoming too small for him, he went to Denver, where his establishment is one of the show places to which the citizens point with pride. He is also interested in the "Famous" store at St. Louis, one of the mammoth concerns of the world. To his shrewdness and lavishness as an advertiser, Dave owes his success as well as his prominence.

Hartford City News   April 10, 1923

David May, former local resident, is now one of the country's leading merchantile men. The people who lived here before 1876 will remember Mr. May. Among his intimate friends of that period are Ollie H. Hiatt, Harl Hiatt, and William Van Cleve. The late Mayer Weiler was one of his old friends, having been for many years a friend of both Mr. and Mrs. Weiler.

Mr. May got his start in Hartford City, coming here without a cent. Mr. May became a partner in one of the early merchantile firms of this city, Kirshbaum, Winters and May. He was so sorely troubled with asthma that he was forced to change climates and he went from this city to Leadville, Colorado, where he was twice elected to county office. He became one of the leading merchants of that thriving mining city and afterwards entered upon a bigger field in Denver.

Mr. May's old friends in this county have watched his career with much interest and they have been much pleased with his rise as one of the country's foremost merchants.

(The beginning of the May Department Store is generally traced to Colorado where David May started his business in the town of Leadville. He had moved west for a climate that was more agreeable to his health. However, we in Blackford County know that David May got his early training and business expertise in Hartford City, Indiana.)

Hartford City News   May 12, 1923

GIVES $1000 TO HOSPITAL

David May former resident and merchant offers to help hospital.
To Equip Laboratory
Money to be used in the establishment of a laboratory—in Hands of Board of Trustees

David May, former well know merchant of this city, now owner of a string of great department stores known as the May Department Stores Company, has written to his old friend, Oliver H. Hiatt, that he is still interested in the welfare of Hartford City and Blackford County although he left the city over fifty years ago.

In a recent letter to Mr. Hiatt, Mr. May states that he is willing to contribute $1000 toward the establishment of a laboratory and equipment for the Blackford County Hospital.

While here, Mr. May was in the merchantile business with Raphael Kirshbaum.

<u>Hartford City News</u>   June 30, 1923

RECEIVES GIFT FOR HOSPITAL. DAVID MAY, OF ST. LOUIS, SENDS GIFT OF $1000 TO BE APPLIED TO LABORATORY FUND.

Oliver H. Hiatt, Saturday morning, received a check for $1000 from David May, head of the David May Department Stores of St. Louis, and a former resident of this city, for the establishment of a laboratory in the Blackford County Hospital, to be known as the David May Laboratory. The money was placed on deposit by Mr. Hiatt in the Citizens State Bank; a suitable plate will be provided to be placed in the laboratory setting forth the names of the donors.

<u>Hartford City Times Gazette</u>   July 27, 1927

TRIBUTE PAID TO MEMORY OF DAVID MAY

St. Louis, Missouri

Work as a "divine obligation" believed in by the Jewish people and exemplified in the character of David May, founder of the May company which has branches in many cities, was the theme of the funeral sermon of Rev. Samuel Sale, rabbi emeritus of Temple Israel here, in the funeral services for May yesterday.

Hundreds of rich and poor, Jews and Gentiles, stood side by side as the services were read. The interment was private.

*David May and the May Company, became the Famous-Barr Company and was known to Indiana residents as the L. S. Ayres Company. In the East the Famous-Barr Company had stores known as Hecht's. In 2005 the stores were sold and became Macy's (Federated Department Stores).

<u>Telegram</u>   January 25, 1894

Messrs. Morris Weiler, of Portland, Chas. Weiler, of Farmland, J. Strauss, of Hicksville, Ohio, A. Weiler, of Indianapolis, and Adolph Weiler of Hartford City, all members of the Weiler Syndicate, of which Steifel's Sons are members, met in annual session at Angola this week, to elect officers and arrange business for the coming year. The syndicate is formed for the purpose of buying goods direct from the manufacturers.

Odds & Ends Book 16, p. 117 (pictures November 19, 1918)

As the doors swing open at 8 o'clock Saturday morning we will start the celebration of the Fiftieth Anniversary of the forming of a partnership between Col. Winters and Raphael Kirshbaum in 1868.

They laid the foundations of this business upon principles of strict integrity, won the confidence of the public and established the good will which this house enjoys today. Later in the history of the institution David May succeeded Col. Winters. But on account of ill health Mr. May was forced to give up active duty and seek the healthful climate of Colorado, where he again embarked in the mercantile business which today has grown to immense proportions, having branches in Denver, St. Louis, Cleveland, Akron, Ohio, and Pittsburgh. When Mr. May withdrew Mr. Abe Weiler became identified with Mr. Kirshbaum and about that time began the real growth of Hartford City and with the broadening out of this store's usefulness. Further progress was constantly strengthened and extended by the Weiler Brothers in succession, Mr. Abe Weiler, Mr. Adolph Weiler and the present M. M. Weiler, who cherishes as a priceless heritage the good will won by years of friendly, helpful service and fair dealings and which is the constant aim to make more permanent. And we hope to make more friends for the store in 1918 than in any of the fifty years that have passed.

As a tribute to the founders and us, an expression of our appreciation of public confidence fairly won and maintained, we shall celebrate this fiftieth year as our GOLDEN YEAR, and in a manner long to be remembered. We believe we can properly refer to the honorable career of the house, but we cannot expect to make any especially strong impression on the public by recounting past achievements alone. Our reasons for celebrating the Golden Year are largely sentimental.

Mayer M. Weiler   History of Blackford County B. G. Shinn, 1914

It is a full half century since the house of Kirshbaum & Weiler was established in Hartford City as a mercantile enterprise with a general stock which was gradually evolved into departments, giving the community its first department store. Only the older residents recall the the Kirshbaum store, for many years ago it was succeeded by the Weiler interests and the Weiler Department Store has long stood pre-eminent in the estimation of the shopping public of Blackford County.

It was in 1864 that the Kirshbaum store was established in Hartford City. In 1866 Mr. David May became a partner and in 1876 Mr. Abe Weiler succeeded Mr. May. Mr. A. R. Weiler bought an interest in 1887, and in 1888 there came into the firm Mr. M. M. Weiler, who succeeded to the interests of Mr. Kirshbaum. At that time the business was organized under the name of A. Weiler & Brothers, and that has ever since continued the business designation of this large store, though some changes have occurred in the personnel. In 1897 (store was built in 1896) was erected the splendid large store at the northeast corner of the public square, on a foundation 100 x 120 feet, three stories high, and all the floor space is occupied by the extensive stock, which is divided into departments, including clothing, millinery, carpets, furniture, men's and women's apparel and all goods required both for city and country trade. The Weiler store has always represented progressive enterprise, has dealt in reliable goods, has used methods for stimulating trade, and the reputation of the house has been behind every article sold over the counters. In 1911 Mr. A. Weiler, who had been head of the firm, died, but the name is still kept. The sole proprietors at present are Mr. Adolph Weiler and M. M. Weiler. The Hartford City store is one of the chain of stores, and this modern principle of merchandising has been carried out with great success by Weiler Brothers. Other stores are located at Portland and Farmland, Indiana, and at Fort Recovery, Ohio. The Hartford City store is under the personal management of Mr. M. M. Weiler. In the busy season eighty people are employed in that large emporium, and taking all the stores together they furnish employment to about two hundred people. Since the Weilers came into the business they have developed it beyond all comparison with its earlier stages, and its capital and volume of trade aggregate four or five times what they did twenty or twenty-five years ago. Each store has its separate buyer and is under separate management.

Mayer M. Weiler, head of the Hartford City store, was born in Bavaria, Germany, of a fine Hebrew family, and is an educated gentleman not only a successful merchant but a public spirited and leading citizen. He was born fifty-three years ago, was reared and educated in his native country, and in 1882 came to the United States, locating at Farmland, Indiana. It was there that he sold his first goods, and then in 1887 came to Hartford City and in the following year became associated with his present business. He was at that time twenty-six years of age, and has long been one of the foremost merchants of Blackford County.

Mr. Weiler was marred at Peru, Indiana, to Nellie Levi, who was born at Peru, and educated in the public schools there. Mr. and Mrs. Weiler have one son, Adolph R. Weiler.

Telegram   May 2, 1900

Mrs. Rosalind Weiler, widow of Isaac Weiler, and mother of the Weiler brothers of this city, died in New York last Saturday, age 74 years. She had eleven children, eight still living: Abe, of Indianapolis; Mrs. Fred Levy, Denver, Colorado; Mrs. Joseph Jacobs, New York City; Mrs. Nathan Winters, Brooklyn; Morris, Portland, Indiana; Charles, Danville, Illinois, Adolph and Mayer, this city.

Telegram   February 14, 1895

Weiler-Levi Nuptials

The Peru Chronicle contains the following account of the Weiler-Levi nuptials at Peru. The marriage of Mayer M. Weiler, of Hartford City, and Miss Nellie Levi was a brilliant event in Jewish circles, and occurred in the spacious parlors of the Bearss hotel. The rooms were beautifully decorated with smilax and begonias and cut flowers, roses and carnations, and palms and potted plants were tastefully arranged on the sideboard and tables. At precisely 7:30 o'clock the bridal procession, greeted by the strains of superb music from the Peru city orchestra stationed at the entrance of the hallway, marched from the back parlor to the center parlor, led by the officiating minister, Rabbi Messing, followed by the bridal pair and their near relatives, halted underneath a floral design of two hearts of white and pink carnations with a border of smilax, where Rabbi Messing performed the ceremony. The groom's best man was Solomon Munter, of Indianapolis. The bride's attendant was her sister, Miss Emma. She was attired in light blue silk, trimmed in real cream lace, and wore a beautiful diamond pendant. The bride wore white duchesse satin trimmed in white point lace, a tulle veil and diamond ornament. Following the ceremony the usual congratulations were extended and about 8 o'clock the guests assembled in the dining room where an elaborate supper had been prepared by Landlord Turpen and plates laid for 150 guests. A splendid menu was spread from which nothing was omitted that is customarily served at wedding feats, including the finest wines and champagne. At 11 o'clock the post prandial speeches had all been made and the feasting was over. Dancing was then commenced in G. A. R. hall, where both old and young assembled to participate in the festivities which were continued until about 3 o'clock this morning, the hour for the departure of the bridal couple on the Wabash train for the east, where they will make a three weeks' trip, visiting the larger cities. They will be at home to their friends at Hartford City at the end of the honeymoon excursion. The couple were the recipients of many costly and handsome gifts. The father of the bride presented them with $500 in gold; Abe Weiler of Indianapolis, a fine house and lot in Hartford City, in which they will reside, and the brother of the bride, Edward Levi, a $400 piano, besides silver and gold table sets. Numerous other useful and ornamental gifts were presented.

Evening News   January 14, 1905

HURRAH! HURRAH! MAYER'S NOW A PA

The happiest man in all the city is Mayer Weiler. Neighbors saw him at an early hour Saturday morning standing on the apex of the roof of his residence waving his hands and crying. Hurrah! Hurrah! I am now a Pa. His voice could be heard for some distance but many could not distinguish the words until they got within three squares. He finally turned a handspring and slid down a lightning rod. It was soon learned that the stork had visited his home about midnight and left a fine baby boy. Mother and child are doing well and it is thought Mayer will be all right in a few days. Grandpa Levi was soon notified at Peru, of the arrival of the heir. Mayer wanted to talk over the Western Union wires and send a telegraph message by the telephone company, but he was in time straightened out and got what he wanted over the right wires.

Evening News   December 12, 1916

RAPHAEL KIRSCHBAUM DIES TUESDAY

Raphael Kirschbaum, 74, prominent Indianapolis business man and founder of the Weiler Bros. store in Hartford City, died at Indianapolis.

Raphael Kirschbaum was born in Fusagenheim, Rheinpfala, Germany. When a lad of 17 years he came to America and started in business at Union City, Indiana. In 1866 he associated himself with Major Winters in what is now the Weiler store, in this city. In 1867, David May purchased the interest of Mr. Winters and the store became Kirschbaum & May, located on the east side of the public square. Later Abram Weiler, who was then associated with Mr. Kirschbaum in the Union City store, came here and purchased the Kirschbaum & May store.

In 1885 Mr. Kirschbaum moved to Indianapolis from Union City and resided there since that time. It was at Indianapolis that he made the bulk of his fortune, in the real estate business, being reputed to have an estate of between $4,000,000 and $5,000,000 at the time of his death. He built the Kirschbaum building on the east side of the square in this city also the building now occupied by the Levy store, at the southwest corner of the public square.

Surviving Mr. Kirschbaum are one son and three daughters, as follows: Bernie Kirschbaum, Mrs. Mose Fisher and Mrs. Albert Rosenthal, all of Indianapolis, and Mrs. Simon Lion, of Washington, D. C.

Mr. Kirschbaum was a man whom wealth did not change. He was the most unpretentious of men and it was this quality as well as his sterling honesty and integrity that endeared him to his friends. He was a man of wide charities, but there was no show with his charity, for he truly lived out the tenet: "Let not thy right hand know what the left hand doeth."

Since Germany did not become a unified country until 1871, many immigrants listed the states from which they came.

GERMANS APPLYING FOR CITIZENSHIP
IN BLACKFORD COUNTY

Name	Date of Arrival	
Andren, John	June 1, 1902	(Austria-Hungary)
Avriganu, Simon	April 8, 1903	(Austria-Hungary)
Barb, John	October 12, 1903	(Austria-Hungary)
Bauer, Jacob	April, 1884	(Wurttemberg)
Bunkker, Charles	October 17, 1860	(Baden)
Cale, Conrad	November 15, 1850	(Hesse-Darmstadt)
Coman, John	November 5, 1902	(Austria-Hungary)
Craymer, Henry	1871	(Oldenberg)
Fichtner, Frank	October 27, 1904	(Germany)
Fischerbock, Christian	May 25, 1860	(Lippe-Detmold)
Fisher, Adolphus	March 15, 1853	(Bavaria)
Fisherback, Frederick	May, 1854	(Germany)
Frey, John	March 13, 1872	(Germany)
Gaga, Gavril	March 8, 1902	(Austria-Hungary)
Guenther, John Emil	May 2, 1896	(Germany)
Horn, Theodore	February 2, 1885	(Hesse-Darmstadt)
Huffman, John	Febrary 2, 1885	(Hesse-Darmstadt)
Hug, Joseph	June 4, 1922	(Germany)
Kaiser, Alois	August 15, 1867	(Wurttemberg)
Kappiss, Franz	July 26, (no year given)	(Wurttemberg)
Kelemen, John	August 19, 1902	(Austria-Hungary)
Kleefisch, Philipp	April 12, 1865	(Prussia)
Korver, John	February 11, 1873	(Bavaria)
Kuttler, Simeon	May 1, 1881	(Wurttemberg)
Lauck, Philip	April 9, 1898	(Germany)
Laux, John	May 3, (no year given)	(Prussia)
Leis, Michael	April 13, 1882	(Germany)
Lungocin, Pavel	May 20, 1902	(Austria-Hungary)
Lunne, Barnhart	November 5, 1866	(Oldenburg)
Marpozan, Jacob	April 21, 1903	(Austria-Hungary)
Miller, Herman	March 19, 1899	(Germany)
Miller, John A. G.	June 1, 1853	(Bavaria)
Nebe, Heinrich	October 25, 1857	(Hanover)
Nicu, Zaharie	November 18, 1904	(Austria-Hungary)
Olt, Adam	July 14, 1877	(Germany)
Ott, George	June 13, 1866	(Bavaria)
Parvu, Nicolae	June 1, 1902	(Austria-Hungary)

Perchang, Eugene	April 4, 1893	(Germany)
Pohl, Emil	December 7, 1906	(Germany)
Porsch, Frederick	July 6, 1891	(Germany)
Potroca, Vasile	March 7, 1903	(Austria-Hungary)
Rosca, Nicolac	November 2, 1903	(Austria-Hungary)
Rusu, David	March 20, 1904	(Austria-Hungary)
Sandor, John	November 10, 1902	(Austria-Hungary)
Sandor, Vasil	November 10, 1902	(Austria-Hungary)
Sauer, Michael	August 28, 1888	(Germany)
Schmidt, Mike	April 12, 1903	(Austria-Hungary)
Schuller, Fred	September 25, 1913	(Austria-Hungary)
Schweier, Emil	December 17, 1893	(Germany)
Shwope, John	October 26, 1882	(Wurttemberg)
Sinerth, Michael	December 3, 1893	(Germany)
Steitz, Peter	March 15, 1848	(Baden)
Stroble, Richard	October 15, 1850	(Germany)
Ureche, Tom	November 15, 1902	(Austria-Hungary)
Ursu, Niculoe	January 2, 1902	(Austria-Hungary)
Wadel, Adam	September 28, 1854	(Hesse-Dermstadt)
Wagener, Mikel	November 15, 1890	(Germany)
Walker, John	June 25, 1872	(Wurttemberg)
Walker, John Frederick	September 15, 1872	(Germany)
Weber, Adam	April 1, 1852	(Prussia)
Weiler, Adolph	June 5, 1880	(Bavaria)
Weiler, David	May 29, 1882	(Rhineland-Palatinate)
Wolf, George	May 13, 1872	(Germany)
Wolf, Herman	August 2, 1893	(Germany)
Yeager, Balser	November 10, 1866	(Hesse-Darmstadt)
Yeager, Henry	January 3, 1855	(Hesse-Darmstadt)
Yunglas, John	July 7, 1860	(Germany)

THE GREEKS

PALACE

—— O F ——

SWEETS

We make our Ice Cream,
Fruits and Candies.

LAMBROS COHEYS

PROPRIETOR

1918 advertisement for Lambrose Coheys candy store
located on South Side of the square.

No *149*

ORIGINAL

UNITED STATES OF AMERICA

Department of Commerce and Labor
BUREAU OF IMMIGRATION AND NATURALIZATION
DIVISION OF NATURALIZATION

DECLARATION OF INTENTION

(Invalid for all purposes seven years after the date hereof)

State of *Indiana* } ss.:
Blackford County. }

In the *Circuit* Court of *Blackford County*

I, *Lambros Coheys*, aged *32* years, occupation *Candy - maker*, do declare on oath affirm that my personal description is: Color *white*, complexion *dark*, height *5* feet *7* inches, weight *140* pounds, color of hair *black*, color of eyes *brown*, other visible distinctive marks *none*

I was born in *Garacide, Greece* on the *5th* day of *October*, anno Domini 1 *887*; I now reside at *Hartford City, Indiana West Wash St*. I emigrated to the United States of America from *Athens, Greece* on the vessel *Austrian American Line* my last foreign residence was *Athens, Greece*.

It is my bona fide intention to renounce forever all allegiance and fidelity to any foreign prince, potentate, state, or sovereignty, and particularly to *Alexander 1 King of Greece*, of which I am now a citizen subject; I arrived at the port of *New York*, in the State Territory District of *New York* on or about the *10* day of *June*, anno Domini 1 906; I am not an anarchist; I am not a polygamist nor a believer in the practice of polygamy; and it is my intention in good faith to become a citizen of the United States of America and to permanently reside therein: SO HELP ME GOD.

Lambros Coheys
(Original signature of declarant.)

[SEAL.]

Subscribed and sworn to before me this *8th* day of *October*, anno Domini 19 *19*

Earl Reasoner,
Clerk of the *Blackford* Court.
By *Lewis Reeves*, Deputy Clerk.

*Lambrose Coheys filed his declaration of intention in 1906
and listed "candy maker" as his occupation.*

Picture of store front—"Palace of Sweets" is shown behind the Gable Hardware fair display.

SOME PLACE TO GO

The Olympia Candy Kitchen

Headquarters for Fine Xmas Box Candies, Home Made Candies, Cigars, Soft Drinks and Hot Fountain Drinks.

SHORT ORDER LUNCH A SPECIALTY

The Olympia Candy Kitchen

S. SIDE SQUARE   LAMBROS]COHEYS, Prop.

This advertisement for the "Olympia Candy Kitchen" appeared in the newspaper in 1916.

Daily Gazette   June 11, 1902

FIRST GREEK IN HISTORY OF COUNTY NATURALIZED

The first Greek ever to be naturalized in Blackford County renounced his allegiance to King George III Monday morning.

He is Frank Kanokoposs and works for Desire Patoux. He is just 21 years old and has been in this country since 1895. His parents still live in Greece and Frank has sent them $200 a year ever since he has been in America. He speaks English readily.

Daily Gazette   December 2, 1901

MEN WEAR SKIRTS AT DAILY TOIL

Men in skirts, and short ones at that, hardly reaching to their knees, can be seen in Hartford City daily.

These men skirt wearers are Greeks employed on the Panhandle grade (Pennsylvania Railroad) who have just come from their native country and have not learned to adopt the pants worn in this country. With the short skirt and queer vest-like garment they use for shirt and coat, they make an odd picture.

About eighty Greeks have been employed by the Pennsylvania company on the grade during the last three months, but twenty-five of them were discharged Saturday as the result of a general fight among the workmen. They had been at work on the south side of the grade near the Lake Erie tracks when one of them who goes by name of "Nick" who thought he was doing more than his share of labor, called the attention of his co-workers to the fact that they were unloading one car while the gang he was with disposed of the contents of three cars. This enraged the shirkers and they began to hurl vulgar names at "Nick" and shovels were up in the air in a moment's time. Peace was brought about before any great harm befell anyone. As soon as Antonios Kanelopulas, the overseer, returned from Chicago Saturday afternoon, the matter was laid before him and as a result, the discharge of over one-third of the unruly Greeks took place.

Antonios Kanelopulas, who is employed as overseer, also acts as interpreter. He speaks fairly good English and is an entertaining speaker. He is a native of Greece, a graduate of several of the leading universities at Athens, and has only resided in this country a short time. He makes Chicago his home where he is treasurer of the Greek Society. The Panhandle company has had "Tony" in their employ for some time and appreciate his services. He is well liked by his fellow workmen.

Kanelopulas regrets very much the mix-up between the workmen which would undoubtedly not have occurred had he not been called away. The pay car reaches here Tuesday and the discharged Greeks will then return to the windy city.

LAMBROSE COHEYS

Lambrose Coheys, a Greek confectioner, came to this city about 1914 and established a candy store known as the Olympia Candy Kitchen. Judging by the product sold, the store must have been very popular with the townsmen.

Mr. Coheys was the first man here to take advantage of the new law which allowed ex-soldiers who were not citizens of the United States to become naturalized with less confusion than ordinary citizens.

In a year or so, Mr. Coheys sold the candy store to George and A. P. Sperou from Warsaw, Indiana and it was renamed Palace of Sweets.

Only two months later the Sperous sold the Palace of Sweets to Mr. and Mrs. Tom Pappas of Chicago, also Greeks. The Sperous returned to Warsaw to be connected with a candy kitchen there owned by their cousin.

When Lambrose Coheys sold his store here, he went to Muncie where he purchased the New London Restaurant, later selling it to Theodore Dardas, his friend. He had businesses at Marion and Wabash, also.

On March 31, 1926 Lambrose Coheys, died in the Flower Mission Annex of the Marion County hospital following an illness of tuberculosis of the throat.

Word of Mr. Cohey's illness was not received in Hartford City until about ten days before his death. A committee from the Elks Lodge, of which he was a member, was sent to his bedside, but his condition was such that little could be done. He was visited on the day of his death by O. P.

Shug, local member of the Elks, Theodore Dardas of Muncie and Thomas Pappas of Wabash, Greek countrymen and business associates. He rallied once during their visit, lifted his head slightly and murmured, "Take me back to Hartford City." These were his only coherent words.

Little is known of the life of Lambrose Coheys. He was a native of Galaxide, Greece and was about 38 years old. He frequently told of his boyhood home in Greece. At one time Coheys was said to have been worth considerable money. He was a good fellow among men, and during the War, gave considerable time and money to making gifts for his Hartford City friends.

His dying wish was that his body be returned here for burial. Hartford City was "home" to the world wanderer and his resting place is near those whom he considered friends.

<u>Evening News</u>   March 30, 1915

FOREIGNERS BUY GROCERY

George H. Turner and wife to Tashi D. Shomboloff, Spiro Gosheff, Apostol P. Rodeff and Tasc Spiroff, consideration $750. This is the grocery store on South Jefferson Street which the enterprising foreigners have been conducting for some time. It was several months ago that they purchased the building but the deed has just been recorded.

PALACE
_____OF_____
SWEETS

We make our Ice Cream.
Fruits and Candies.

LAMBROSE COHEYS

PROPRIETOR
(1918)

SOME PLACE TO GO
The Olympia Candy Kitchen

——————

Headquarters for Fine Xmas Box Candies,
Home Made Candies, Cigars, Soft
Drinks and Hot Fountain Drinks.
SHORT ORDER LUNCH A SPECIALTY
The Olympia Candy Kitchen
S. SIDE SQUARE   LAMBROSE COHEYS, Prop.
(1916)

GREEK IMMIGRANTS APPLYING FOR CITIZENSHIP IN BLACKFORD COUNTY

Name	Date of Arrival
Agapitos, George	March 3, 1907
Alafandes, James	March 15, 1908
Alex, Mack	October 1, 1909
Alfante, James	March 15, 1908
Andrew, Gus	March 30, 1908
Babalis, Christ	June 2, 1907
Babalis, Peter	April 25, 1906
Chucalas, Andrias	June 20, 1906
Chucalas, Jion	March 14, 1908
Coheys, Lampras	June 10, 1906
Demos, John	April 6, 1904
Diniacos, John	May 14, 1905
Dordas, Theodore	October 8, 1910
Gaimis, Gus	April 21, 1906
Gaimis, John	March 29, 1907
Gigikos, Bill	November 13, 1906
Huvardas, Athan	August 15, 1906
Johns, John	October 9, 1907
Knollos, Frank	July 15, 1895
Koleniates, Soterious	April 5, 1907
Lefft, William V.	April 6, 1904
Nikos, Spiros	September 10, 1909
Padalfonios, Pelopidos	September 1, 1909
Panagopoulos, William	September 15, 1903
Panagos, Christ	April 2, 1907
Panagos, Peter	May 2, 1909
Pappas, Thomas	April 25, 1902
Pappis, Christ	April 2, 1907
Pollits, Sam	March 15, 1903
Ponopoulos	October 10, 1904
Poulosdavis, George	April 2, 1907
Rigos, Aristidis	September 11, 1909
Rigos, Christ	April 2, 1906
Roumbaka, Haris	August 15, 1907
Spiropoulos, Spiros	May 10, 1904
Stafas, Bill	April 2, 1906
Stassines, Gus	November 14, 1907

Stath, Gus	June 29, 1908
Tismelis, Manolis	September 25, 1909
Vasilakapoulos, Peter	September 3, 1907
Zeppos, Jason Antonion	April 15, 1898

THE GYPSIES

FIRST OF THE SEASON

A Band of Gypsies Encamped in the Bottoms Near the Pulp Mills

A small band of gypsies have been encamped near the Hartford City Paper mills. They belong to the tribe which makes its headquarters near Dayton in the winter months and in the summer time travels leisurely from town to town at its own sweet will. The band at present in the suburbs is typical of the race, swarthy of complexion, indolent except when the opportunity offers to cheat or filch, and speaking a gibberish that is a mixture of Romany and slang of thieves.

As in most gypsy camps every woman is a fortune teller. It is astonishing how the fortune tellers pad their cunning with actual information. Every sign of simpering miss, every hope of country swain, reveals a secret to increase the store of uncanny knowledge in the gypsy memory. For wise and alert victims the crone possesses century-old platitudes which apply in every emergency. By almost imperceptible indications in mood, manner, complexion, look or speech she seizes information and imparts revelation. She wishes to be known as a witch and she comes as near being one as the nineteenth century will permit.

The women have ample time to ply their trade of fortune telling. There is little housekeeping to be done. The beds are nothing but cots. There is little dusting and no sweeping and the amenities of ordinary society affect them not. All the women smoke pipes. The children grow up in the light of the example of their elders. There are no schools and no instruction beyond what is to be found in the experiences of life. They grow with the vigor and elasticity of nature. The girls are taught to cook and tell fortunes; the boys to hunt, fish and trade horses. Family life is simple, but notwithstanding conditions approaching vagabondage, the family is respected and the marriage tie as sacred as in more polished society.

The most glib-tongued and shrewd of the male gypsies are horse-traders, who by a cursory glance into the mouth, by rubbing his shins, or by viewing him with squinting eyes, are able to reveal much knowledge of the animal. No sane gypsy was ever known to get the worst of a horse trade.

The longevity of the gypsy is not so great as that of the women. The lack of stern principles, of exercise, notwithstanding the free outdoor life, joined by personal untidiness indulged in from youth, leave their traces. The youngsters who lounge about camp are particularly unprepossessing. Their slouch hats, buttonless jackets, unkempt hair and grimy visages repel rather than attract. Then they are excessive users of tobacco and liquors.

The gypsy is indeed a singular phenomenon. Born into the life, they seldom leave it. From the time of their earliest recorded ancestor in Hindostan they have been nomadic. They have escaped the influence of the successive civilizations of the world's history. Their name comes through the belief, prevalent at one time, that they were originally from Egypt. They adapt themselves only as far as necessary to the customs of the country in which they are. Everywhere they are as free as the air they breathe.

In this country the number who travel and abide in tents has greatly increased within the last few years and they travel from Canada to Texas. They still have many of the Romany words but they have acquired a practical understanding of the language of America.

Daily Times Gazette   June 17, 1900

Three Gypsy Men Take Place of Dead Horse

Three dusty gypsies, pushing and pulling at an old ramshackle wagon within which members of their families were seated, passed through the edge of town.

One of the men was walking between the shafts and the other two were pushing at the rear of the conveyance. Three women and several children were inside the wagon. The gypsies said that they had walked all the way from Dunkirk where their horse died. They said that they were unable to purchase another and for this reason had to act as their own beast of burden. All three of the men were nearly exhausted. The man in front was scarcely able to walk because his feet were so badly swollen. They were bleeding freely. Kind farmers made up a purse for them and presented them with old shoes and clothes. The gypsies have to beg enough money to buy a cheap horse and farmers south of town donated freely.

<u>Evening News</u>   April 21, 1902

"We'll give ye two cents and a dance for them bananas," said the oldest looking one of a trio of juvenile gypsies this morning to George Laine, clerk at the Ayres Grocery, and he pointed to a number of black bananas. "Go ahead with your dance," said Mr. Laine, and the trio, two boys and a girl, with long black hair and Indian-like features, went out on the sidewalk and danced a jig to the music of a mouth organ blown by the oldest one, apparently the leader. Several pedestrians threw them pennies. Then they got their bananas and went down Main Street a short distance and sitting down on the curb proceeded to devour the bananas. They attracted considerable attention.

<u>Evening News</u>   April 28, 1902

THE GYPSY QUEEN

Evansville, Ind.—A handsome monument has just been erected here to the memory of the Gypsy queen and other gypsies who are buried in Oak Hill cemetery. The gypsies of the United States regard Evansville as their headquarters, and a few years ago when their queen died at Dayton, Ohio, her remains were brought here for burial, and over 5,000 gypsies from various parts of the country came here to attend the services.

Since the death of the queen several others of the tribe have died and have been brought here for burial. When the queen died her wagon in which she traveled, as well as all its belongings were burned according to the gypsy custom, and the ashes scattered on her grave.

The gypsies in this section are now moving in the direction of Dayton, where they will attend the funeral of one of their tribe.

<u>Daily Times Gazette</u>   August 13, 1906

GYPSIES HAD TO HIKE

A gang of dirty gypsy fortune tellers struck this city Monday and became such a nuisance that Marshal Nelson Worley ordered them to leave. They not only begged but they were insulting in their actions and talk. One of the tribe entered the Lieber & Campbell hardware store and even approached a dummy and asked him if he wanted his fortune told. She kept tugging at his arm and when the wooden man, who was dressed up for an advertisement, did not respond she began to cuss him. Still he gave no heed and when she discovered that the object she was talking to was not a real man, she swore at him like a trooper and left the store amid the laughing and jeering of the clerks.

Daily Times Gazette   May 19, 1906

GYPSY SKINNED THE COLORED 'CHAMPEEN'

Dusky Maiden from Sunny Italy Showed Tim Harlan a New Trick

Tim Harlan, the well known colored pugilist and blacksmith was victimized by one of the members of the gypsy tribe which visited this city Friday. Tim was caught off his guard by one of the dusky fortune tellers and was landed in the corner and compelled to give in to her plea to read his fortune.

It was first necessary to cross her palm with a coin and then Tim was asked to place a five dollar gold piece in the corner of a handkerchief and tie it very tight. He followed the instructions and then handed the woman the handkerchief. The gypsy took the handkerchief and placed in it Tim's "championship" belt, telling him to leave it there until 2 o'clock Saturday and he would always meet with a good fortune. The woman left him and after wearing the handkerchief for more than an hour, Tim became suspicious and pulled it out only to find that the money had disappeared. He is on the warpath and swears vengeance on the next teller that comes his way.

Daily Times Gazette   August 14, 1906

GYPSIES TOOK CAKES, PIES, BREAD AND ALL

Filthy Tribe of Thieving Nomads were Bluffed by Bill Bradford

It is well known that the band of gypsies that infested this city Monday were run out of town or they would have carried away half the city.

They were the biggest bunch of thieving females and highway robbers that ever struck Hartford City. In nearly every store they visited they stole something, and on the South Side successfully held up Mrs. Omar

Dekeyser's bread wagon and robbed it of all the bread, pies, and cakes. They attempted the same trick with Bill Bradford, who drives the Hively bakery delivery wagon, but Bill stood pat and threatened to whip the whole dirty tribe if they didn't skidoo in a hurry.

<u>Daily Times Gazette</u>   December 3, 1906

GYPSY CAMP RAIDED BY MARSHAL WORLEY

Dusky Tribe Set up Housekeeping on Dr. Davisson Farm

Some people say that a gypsy won't steal, but Dr. Davisson caught one in his corn field Monday that had the goods on him.

Having been notified by a neighbor that a band of twelve horse traders was camping on his farm just east of the city and was stealing his crops and destroying the fences to make kindling wood for a fire, the doctor secured the aid of Marshal Worley and drove out to his farm to drive them away.

When they reached the place they caught one of the tribe red-handed. He was in the corn field with a sack when the marshal espied him and at the command, "Throw Up Your Hands," he dropped his corn and ran like a deer. After an exciting foot race the marshal overtook him and marched him back to the camp where he was exhibited as a captive to the rest of the tribe. Several bushels of corn had been gathered from the field and hauled to camp where it lay scattered around on the ground. Threatened with arrest for stealing, the gypsies paid for the damage they had done and were given just thirty minutes to pack up and leave. The time allowed them was of sufficient length for in less than fifteen minutes they were well on their way to the next camp.

Besides the twelve gypsies there were about fifteen horses and these had been turned into the pasture field. The farm is not tenanted and the tribe had taken full possession and were making themselves at home when the officer raided them.

<u>Evening News</u>   August 26, 1916

RECOVER MONEY FROM GYPSIES

The worst outfit of thieves which has struck this city for some time blew in Saturday morning when a gypsy band hit town. During the gang's short stay here they relieved residents of $5.15. The thefts were discovered just as the nomads were ready to leave town, however, and the money recovered.

The gypsies came to this city from the west and stopped at a number of the business houses in West Washington Street to tell fortunes. At the S. L. Stephenson store, one of the women in the party stopped and asked to tell the proprietor's fortune. The business man declined. Mr. Stephenson at the time was checking up the proceeds of Friday, preparatory to going to the bank. Joseph Manning, drayman, came to the door at that time with several packages for the harness store and Mr. Stephenson placed all the money with the exception of a $5 bill in a sack. The note he put in one of his pockets, after which he ordered the woman to leave his store.

About fifteen minutes later Mr. Stephenson looked for the bill and found that it had disappeared. He then informed the police and a search was made for the gypsy. The woman attempted to deny the theft, but finally, at the order of the mayor, gave the $5 bill to Mr. Stephenson.

The gang was then ordered to leave the city. A short time later it was learned that one of the women in the party had also taken fifteen cents from the pocketbook of Arthur Mullins. While telling the fortune of Mullins, against his wishes, the woman persuaded him to allow her to put her fingers in his purse, saying that she would bring the owner good luck in financial matters. Four jitneys reposed in Arthur's pocketbook and three of these stuck to the woman's fingers for some unexplainable reason. Mullins found he was minus and nabbed the woman, forcing her to pay back the money.

HOBOES
TRAMPS
AND BUMS

HOBO – a migratory worker, vagrant, tramp.
TRAMP – one who travels about on foot doing odd jobs or begging.
BUM – a dissolute or worthless person living by sponging from people.
VAGRANT – a person who wanders from place to place especially one without a regular job, supporting himself by begging.

(Webster's New World Dictionary)

Evening News   February 12, 1894

Almost every day during the cold winter months a newspaper office is besieged by tramps who announce themselves by "Please, Mister, can I have some newspapers?" They are never refused. The poorly clad fellows take them with thanks. They put the papers around their arms, legs, and chest to keep out the cold winter winds. In this way the tramp makes up for the lack of an overcoat or heavy clothes.

Evening News   February 21, 1894

Two tramps this morning engaged in a miniature bread riot in the north part of town. One of them by dint of industrious foraging had secured an assortment of grub which he refused to divide with the other who had been too lazy even to beg. The latter then grabbed a fence paling and beat his more enterprising brother in a diversity until he dropped the "handout" and ran. When last seen the bum with the fence paling was serenely enjoying the fruits of his partner's enterprise, while the latter was making his painful way to a locality where he might ply his avocation in peace.

Tramps have become so numerous that some of them find it necessary to offer other pleas than hunger as reasons why they should be fed. One of the knights of the road with an arm done up in a sling got a square meal on the strength of being crippled. The lady of the house was sympathetic and observing this, the tramp made a successful appeal for money. The lady happened to be downtown later on, when she saw her tramp minus the sling, come reeling out of a saloon. There was nothing the matter with his arm and then money he begged had gone for drink.

Evening News   April 7, 1894

A HOBO HIGH ROLLER

The hoboes who make their headquarters in this town are discussing a member of the tramp fraternity who most of them have encountered in their trips over the Panhandle Railroad. This hobo differs from his class in that he is a high roller. He wears elegant clothes, flashes a diamond ring and displays a roll of money that a banker would be afraid to carry. The tourists who have seen him may be mistaken in their judgment of the man's diamond but they do know money when they see it and they are simply dazed by the mysterious tramp's splendor. The high roller passed through here last night in a Panhandle freight car, and a Hartford tourist who came this way in the same car says that he flashed his diamond and his roll, while strapped to his waist was a gun as long as a horse pistol. He said he was going to Converse. The fraternity do not know what to make of him although most of them are agreed that he is a crook. They think he must be "daffy" too or he would not make such arrogant display of his wealth when consorting with bums who have been hoping to catch him napping and despoil him of it.

Daily Gazette   April 21, 1902

Other countries have their outcasts and vagrants, but none of them have anything like the American tramp. He is an oddity and inimitable in his originality and nerve.

Telegram   February 11, 1904

SEASON OF THE HOBO IS NEAR

There are hoboes and hoboes, says a man who has had dealings with the outcasts since the panic of '73. Some are vicious and brutal, others possess mean little traits, while a few are good-natured, harmless creatures. To one who has not investigated the mysteries of tramp life, it will surprise them to know that social distinctions are maintained by hoboes. A member of the aristocratic class is called John Yeg. He is known as a professional bum, who refuses to work under any consideration. He generally holds down one stretch of railroad, and plies his trade in the towns along its line.

Panhandling, begging on the streets, is his graft. The money which he receives is spent for booze, which is drunk at a camp outside the town.

Another class is known as the bingle bum. His distinguishing feature is a weakness for work—that is, he will work once in a while. It is generally this kind of hobo who helps at harvest time, picks peaches in Michigan and grapes and hops in New York state. He is tolerated by the upper class, but is not allowed to partake of the feast at their camps. A mush faker is another kind. His trade is mending umbrellas and drinking bad whisky. The lowest kind of bum known on the road is the pig tail, or town bum, he who has a home and leaves it only to return in a few weeks. He is despised by all the others, and life is made miserable for him.

The hoboes possess a language of their own, and one who is not initiated is unable to grasp the meaning of half what they say. Some of the best known terms: A lump is a couple of pieces of bread and butter wrapped in paper; a section is a lunch with a hot cup of coffee eaten upon the back porch; a set-down, or to swing your leg 'neath the mahogany, is to be invited inside and to enjoy a full meal; a benny is an overcoat; a fogy, a poorhouse; a stop, a jail. There are hundreds of terms just such as these that are daily on the road.

<u>Hartford City News</u>   March 26, 1931

THREE TRAMPS SENT OUT OF CITY

"The world owes me a living, and by ____, I want something to eat!" were the curt words offered Mrs. Arthur Hollis at the Hollis Grocery by one of the itinerants who have for the past three weeks been living in a dug-out near the McDowell Lumber camp, east Franklin Street.

Mrs. Hollis, alone at the grocery, and fearing the three would use force if she failed to comply with the demand, gave them bacon and coffee, but it proved their undoing. The next morning police officials ordered them to leave the city and never return.

According to information given officers by the residents in the east portion of the city, the three men have been "working" the city for several days, and have on several occasions, caused considerable trouble. The three have been living in an improvised earth covered shack made from empty barrels and loose lumber.

THE IRISH,
ENGLISH, WELSH,
AND SCOTTISH

THE MECCA

— SPORTSMEN'S HEADQUARTERS —

"That's Pat"

The Man Who Made "Puritan Rye" and "Harper Rye" Famous in Hartford City

Marion Beer On Tap

THE MECCA

PAT DELANEY, Proprietor

North Side Square,   Hartford City, Indiana

With 24 saloons located in Hartford City in 1902, Pat Delaney, an Irishman, operated his saloon on the north side of the square.

Many immigrants came to work on railroads. This picture is from our photo collection showing laborers but no other identification appears with the photo.

Laying a gas pipeline was another source of employment for workers in the County.

The Tool House Oil Company employees. Boss was Elmer Clair. Will Schultz and Harve Endsley are only workers identified.

<u>Telegram</u>   February 26, 1891

Mrs. Alice Timmons, mother of Mike and Peter Timmons, died last Friday. She was over 90 years old. She was a native of Ireland and came to the country in 1874 in the spring. Burial was in the North Cemetery Monday.

<u>The Daily Gazette</u>   March 17, 1902

At 11 o'clock tonight when Michael Timmons closes the doors of his little saloon on East Washington Street, he will retire from 23 years of active service.

While he conducted the business on different lines than any other man in the liquor trade, nevertheless, he has amassed a fortune.

During all the time he conducted a saloon he never lost a day on account of sickness. He never hired a bartender, and the total value of the furniture in his place is not $5. He was never known to be intoxicated and was never arrested for keeping open after hours or on Sunday. During the summer he used no ice and the amount of inventory on hand at no time exceeded $100. His rent cost him $15 a month, and during the 23 years he has been there he has paid $7,130 to his landlord. Had he purchased the place 23 years ago, he could have secured it for $800. It was sold to the Miller Brewing Company last week for $5000. In dimensions it is 25 x 120 feet.

<u>Evening News</u>   August, 1902

Those who travel much by railroad these days cannot have failed to observe the change in the nationality of the men engaged in railroad construction and repair. Formerly the Emerald Isle supplied the men who dug the canals, graded and ballasted the railroads and kept them in repair after the rails were laid. Now on the northern roads the Italians, with a sprinkling of Greeks, make up the greater part of the construction force.

The question is asked, "What has become of the Irish?" It is certain that few of them have returned to Ireland. It is likewise certain that they have largely withdrawn from railroad work. An investigation, however, will disclose that many an Irishman who formerly worked at railroad construction and as a section hand after the road was constructed has been advanced a peg. The former Irish immigrant will be found on the farm, which he owns, at the head of various business enterprises, in politics and on the police force, gracing every station he occupies with the peculiar adaptability of the Irish race. In Blackford County there are many instances of this and it is so all over the country. The Irishman is progressive; he is easily assimilated and he becomes an American citizen in spirit shortly after he lands and a citizen in fact as soon as the law will permit him to do so. It is a saying that an Irishman is a great man in every country but his own. He is certainly a power in the United States, which he helps to govern as a statesman, and to rule, as a policeman.

Daily Times Gazette   April 21, 1906

CAME FROM IRELAND TO START SALOON

Mike Timmons came direct to Hartford City from Donnegan County, Ulster, Ireland about 30 years ago and for 7 years worked at day labor on the Lake Erie, since which time he has owned and conducted a saloon in Hartford City continuously, except for a year after the burning of "Rat Row." Mike says he came here because of his brother, James, and James came with Hubbard Spoke factory from Sandusky, Ohio.

Mike says that when he began business the government license was $25. Then the county license went to $100. Lawyer W. A. Bonham got him his first license and charged him $50, which was the established fee until Lawyer Williams went to several saloons and offered to do the work for $10, which put Bonham and other lawyers out of that business and $10 has been the price ever since.

He owns a fine home on South Jefferson street and about a year ago bought the frame business room opposite his place of business.

* The Timmons home was located at 537 South Jefferson in 1906; the saloon was at 112 East Washington Street.

<u>Daily Times Gazette</u>   July 14, 1906

SAID TO BE OLDEST MAN IN COUNTY

"Uncle" John Hallecie, whose funeral was held at the Catholic Church Thursday, was probably the oldest resident in Blackford County.

His exact age is not known but his most intimate friends state that he was not far from the century mark if not more than 100 years old.

He was born in Kerry County, Ireland and came to America many years ago. He had lived in Blackford County 51 years. He was known in Ireland by the late John Cronin, Sr., who always said, when discussing Mr. Hallecie's age, that at the time, he was quite a young man while Cronin was still in knee trousers.

Mr. Cronin was 86 years old at the time of his death. That was three years ago and if he were living now he would be 89 years old. Mr. Hallacie was at least fifteen years older than Mr. Cronin which would make him 104.

Friends are contemplating writing to Ireland to ascertain his exact age. It can be easily told as a record is kept of all births in that country.

<u>Evening News</u>   December 13, 1907

AGED JOHN HOGAN DIES AT HIS DAUGHTER'S HOME

Veteran of Civil War and Highly Respected by the Community in Which He Lived

After a week's illness with pneumonia and infirmities of old age John Hogan passed to his last reward at 2 a.m. Friday at the home of his daughter, Mrs. Murt O'Connell, 700 South Pearl Street.

Mr. Hogan was born in Ireland, March 17, 1825. He came to America when a lad of sixteen years. When war was declared between North and South he joined the 128th Indiana Volunteer Infantry and served as a soldier throughout the war in General Hovey's division. At the close of the war he took up residence in Hartford City and lived here until death. He was a good citizen and well thought of by his fellow townsmen.

Until recent years Mr. Hogan was a member of Jacob Stahl Post G. A. R. The G. A. R. members will attend the funeral in a body.

His children are Edwin, William, James, and George Hogan and Mrs. Mary O'Connell.

JOHN CRONIN AND MARY TRANT

Taken from <u>Sure "N" Begorra, Your Name is Cronin</u> (A Family History of the Descendents of John Cronin formerly of Killdomy Parish, County Kerry, Ireland) by F. Patrick Cronin, Jr. and F. Patrick Cronin, Sr., 1978.

From discussions with various Cronin relatives, I am led to believe that John must have resided for a number of years in the Piqua-Urbana vicinity and must have been well known by Irish families of these communities. John married Mary Trant of Piqua on April 17, 1853.

This John Cronin/Mary Trant marriage not only led to the introduction of the Cronin strain to Indiana, but as well produced the first native born Cronin descendents of Ireland in the United States.

On January 29, 1865, John purchased a one hundred and sixty acre farm, known as the Charles Oxer farm, located one mile west of the small community of Mollie Station, in Blackford County. The farm was located about four miles northeast of Hartford City. Here they lived a pioneer life.

John and Mary were to have nine children during their marriage: James, Michael, Timothy John, Jeremiah Patrick, William Nicholas, Maurice Charles; twin sister to Maurice Charles, died in infancy; Ellen Deborah and David N.

IRISH APPLYING FOR CITIZENSHIP
IN BLACKFORD COUNTY

Name	Date of Arrival
Adams, John	August 15, 1840
Arnold, George	September 30, 1851
Benson, Patrick	April 27, 1848
Breen, Richard	December 4, 1865
Cannon, John	January 7, 1851
Carley, John	August 15, 1865
Carley, Michael	1872
Carley, Patrick Jr.	September, 1872
Carley, Peter	September 9, 1872
Casey, Patrick	May 29, 1863
Cashman, Daniel	January 1, 1852
Cassa, Michael	May 29, 1863
Casson, Patrick	July 1, 1864
Cavaghan, John	March, 1875
Cavana, John	October 15, 1847
Clahasey, Thomas	November 15, 1850
Connelly, John	May 15, 1851
Connor, Michael	November 1, 1852
Cramurans, Patrick	March 15, 1863
Croghan, Thomas	May 20, 1848
Cronin, Michael	May 3, 1852
Crowley, Timothy	May 17, 1853
Crutty, Martin	December 25, 1850
Curran, John	August 20, 1857
Cusack, Laurence	November 15, 1848
Dailey, James	January 17, 1855
Davis, Thomas	August 15, 1853
Donoghue, John	1854
Dowling, John	August 16, 1862
Doyle, John	December 4, 1848
Drishen, Michael	July 22, 1847
Dwire, Thomas	January 15, 1847
Fenerty, James	November 9, 1864
Finn, Peter	May 15, 1848
Forbes, John	August 15, 1847
Gafney, Andrew	May 23, 1862
Gaughen, James	June 1, 1886

Gavaghan, John	March, 1875
Gavin, Michael	July 22, 1862
Geran, Jeremiah	October 27, 1862
Gleeson, Matthew	June 22, 1840
Griffin, Patrick	June 28, 1855
Hagan, John	October 20, 1843
Hall, William	October 22, 1903
Handley, Michael	July 3, 1848
Harley, William	September 18, 1852
Harvey, Thomas	October 13, 1867
Haslett, William	May, 1885
Hesser, Dennis	June 20, 1865
Hesser, John	June 20, 1865
Higgins, Daniel	July 15, 1851
Hines, Michael	1855
Hogan, Dennis	May 15, 1853
Hogan, Thomas	December 1, 1863
Hogan, Thomas	July 12, 1865
Hurly, Garrett	September 13, 1863
Jennings, Thomas	April 20, 1864
Karns, Henry	March, 1882
Kearney, John	February 4, 1852
Keating, Patrick	July 31, 1847
Keefe, Daniel	December 24, 1854
Kenedy, James	July, 1861
Kennedy, Daniel	July 7, 1855
Kerrigan, Michael	April 15, 1860
Kiefe, Thomas	July 13, 1848
Lacy, Martin	May 12, 1847
Maloney, Daniel	November 25, 1852
Maloney, John	November 25, 1852
Manney, Patrick	November 15, 1852
Marone, John	December 7, 1851
Martin, Thomas	May 27, 1864
Maxwell, Thomas	May 4, 1868
McGuire, Terrance	March 25, 1861
McHugh, Andrew	January 1, 1853
McKenna, John	1848
McLaughlin, Michael	June 15, 1858
McLaughlin, Thomas	May 3, 1847
McMahon, Martin	June 25, 1849

McDonald, Peter	May 7, 1857
Meara, Stephen	October 1, 1861
Miller, Thomas	October 4, 1850
Muldoon, James	April 14, 1844
Mulreed, John	------
Murphey, William	September 15, 1857
Murphy, Michael	August 7, 1861
Murry, Richard	October 15, 1845
Mycanthy, Thomas	July 18, 1861
Negle, Patrick	May 15, 1844
Nelson, William	May 15, 1844
Nolen, John	June 1, 1854
O'Brien, Thomas	May 15, 1845
O'Connell, Morty	January 15, 1845
O'Connor, Robert	June 12, 1888
O'Donnell, Michael	October 15, 1847
O'Reilly, James	May 10, 1882
Peacock, Thomas	May 18, 1868
Powers, James	September 20, 1846
Quirk, Jeremiah	April 21, 1860
Redman, Thomas	May 15, 1855
Redmond, John	June 15, 1855
Rhine, John	December 18, 1848
Riley, Christopher	May 1, 1862
Roch, John	July 2, 1863
Ryan, James	May 20, 1868
Senot, Patrick	December 15, 1850
Shauvelen, Pat	June 1, 1852
Shea, Bartholomew	July 15, 1840
Shea, Jeremiah	May 15, 1857
Shea, Michael	August 21, 1864
Shea, Michael	August 2, 1848
Shean, Morris	March 23, 1863
Sheriden, Michael	October 15, 1872
Stack, Thomas	July 25, 1847
Sullivan, John	August, 1865
Sullivan, John	May 20, 1847
Sullivan, John	August 28, 1864
Sullivan, John O.	May 5, 1845
Sullivan, Thomas	February 3, 1852
Sullivan, William J.	June 12, 1851

Timmons, George	July 22, 1870
Timmons, James	July 5, 1865
Timmons, James	April, 1874
Timmons, Michael	April 14, 1874
Timmons, Patrick	April 14, 1874
Timmons, Peter	April 15, 1874
Walsh, Michael	July 12, 1850
Walters, Timothy	June 24, 1863
Warren, John	May 7, 1862
Welch, Michael	November 26, 1851
Welsh, James	March 1, 1853
Willoughby, Robert	August 21, 1870

IMMIGRANTS FROM ENGLAND, WALES, AND SCOTLAND

Name	Date of Arrival	
Bemrose, William	April 27, 1848	(England)
Bevan, James	November 27, 1859	(Wales)
Billings, Maurice	August 20, 1890	(England)
Brown, Samuel	March 31, 1889	(England)
Creiley, Pat	July 2, 1896	(England)
Davis, John	July 28, 1894	(Wales)
Davis, Thomas	March 20, 1897	(Wales)
Dunnett, William	June 14, 1909	(Scotland)
England, John	May 20, 1845	(England)
Gentlemen, Nicholas	-------	(England)
Gilbert, Ben	July 5, 1891	(England)
Gordon, Ross	June 20, 1868	(Scotland)
Griffiths, Daniel	July 20, 1894	(Wales)
Holcroft, Thomas	April, 1848	(England)
Hudsmith, George	August 4, 1884	(England)
Hutchsmith, George	August, 1884	(England)
Johnston, Hugh	April 18, 1889	(England)
Jones, David	July 6, 1895	(Wales)
Jones, Thomas	July 6, 1895	(Wales)
Kates, Richard	July 15, 1850	(England)
McFegan, James	June 2, 1889	(Scotland)
Miller, Peter	1852	(Scotland)
Morgan, Isaac	March 17, 1896	(Wales)
Morton, Henry	May 3, 1851	(England)

O'Neill, William	May 5, 1888	(Wales)
Petty, John	October 1, 1855	(England)
Reese, William	August 15, 1882	(Wales)
Richards, David	September 3, 1891	(Wales)
Schneider, Fred	May 12, 1893	(England)
Stanford, George	March 15, 1846	(England)
Tasker, Thomas	April 2, 1910	(England)
Thomas, David	August 20, 1896	(Wales)
Thomas, Samuel	April 24, 1897	(Wales)
Watkins, David	April 27, 1897	(Wales)
Wellington, William	March 7, 1896	(Wales)
Wilhelm, George	September 22, 1892	(England)
Williams, Edwin	September 24, 1858	(Wales)
Williams, James	May 24, 1898	(Wales)

THE ITALIANS

UNITED STATES OF AMERICA

DECLARATION OF INTENTION
(Invalid for all purposes seven years after the date hereof)

No. 187

State Of Indiana
County Of Blackford } ss:

In the Blackford Circuit Court
of Blackford County at Hartford City

(1) My full, true, and correct name is Marie Grazia Cifelli Di-Cicco

(2) My present place of residence is 417E. 2nd.Hartford City Blackford ...occupation is Housewife

(4) I am 51 years old. (5) I was born on July 15, 1890 in Macchia Valfortore Italy

(6) My personal description is as follows: Sex female, color White, complexion Light, color of eyes Blue, color of hair Brown, height 5 feet 2 inches, weight 135 pounds; visible distinctive marks None

race Italian, present nationality Italian

(7) I am married; the name of my wife or husband is Filippo Antonio Di-Cicco were married on Oct 24,1910 at Macchia Italy he or she was born at Macchia Italy on September 13,1890 and entered the United States at New York New York on April 10,1914 for permanent residence in the United States and now resides at Hartford City, Indiana

(8) I have six children and the name, sex, date and place of birth, and present place of residence of each of said children who is living, are as follows:
Innie Gennett, female, Feb4,1915, Hartford City, Indiana. Hartford City,In
Frank Chick, male, Apr.1,1916
Sam Chick, Jun.20,1918

(9) My last place of foreign residence was Macchia Valfortore Italy (10) I emigrated to the United States from Naples Italy (11) My lawful entry for permanent residence in the United States was at New York New York under the name of Marie Grazia Cifelli Di-Cicco on August 1,1913 on the SS Canada

(12) Since my lawful entry for permanent residence I have not been absent from the United States, for a period or periods of 6 months or longer, as follows:

DEPARTED FROM THE UNITED STATES			RETURNED TO THE UNITED STATES		
Port	Date (Month, day, year)	Vessel or Other Means of Conveyance	Port	Date (Month, day, year)	Vessel or Other Means of Conveyance

(13) I have not heretofore made declaration of intention: No. .... on .... at .... in the ....

(14) It is my intention in good faith to become a citizen of the United States and to reside permanently therein. (15) I will, before being admitted to citizenship, renounce absolutely and forever all allegiance and fidelity to any foreign prince, potentate, state, or sovereignty of whom or which at the time of admission to citizenship I may be a subject or citizen. (16) I am not an anarchist; nor a believer in the unlawful damage, injury, or destruction of property, or sabotage; nor a disbeliever in or opposed to organized government; nor a member of or affiliated with any organization or body of persons teaching disbelief in or opposition to organized government. (17) I certify that the photograph affixed to the duplicate and triplicate hereof is a likeness of me and was signed by me.
I do swear (affirm) that the statements I have made and the intentions I have expressed in this declaration of intention subscribed by me are true to the best of my knowledge and belief. SO HELP ME GOD.

Marie her Frank Di Cicco
(Original and true signature of declarant without abbreviation, also other name if used)

Subscribed and sworn to (affirmed) before me in the form of oath shown above in the office of the Clerk of said Court, at Hartford City, Indiana this .... day of March .... anno Domini 19 42 hereby certify that

Certification No. .... from the Commissioner of Immigration and Naturalization, showing the lawful entry for permanent residence of the declarant above named on the date stated in this declaration of intention, has been received by me, and that the photograph affixed to the duplicate and triplicate hereof is a likeness of the declarant.

[SEAL]

Clerk of the Blackford Circuit Court.

By .... Deputy Clerk.

Declaration of intention Marie Di-Cicco—An Italian family who came to Blackford County in 1914.

Form 2203

UNITED STATES OF AMERICA

Department of Commerce and Labor
BUREAU OF IMMIGRATION AND NATURALIZATION
DIVISION OF NATURALIZATION

DECLARATION OF INTENTION

(Invalid for all purposes seven years after the date hereof)

State of Indiana
Blackford County } ss:

In the Circuit Court of Blackford County

I, Filippo Antonio Di Cicco, aged 37 years, occupation Laborer, do declare on oath that my personal description is: Color white, complexion fair, height 5 feet 5 inches, weight 140 pounds, color of hair Dark brown, color of eyes brown other visible distinctive marks scar center forehead, scar on left cheek : I was born in Macchia Val fortore, Italy, on the 13 day of September, anno Domini 1890 : I now reside at 417 E. 2nd St., Hartford City, Indiana I emigrated to the United States of America from Naples, Italy on the vessel do not remember name of vessel; my last foreign residence was Macchia Val fortore, Italy I am married. It is name of my wife is Maria Grazia Cifello Di Cicco, she was born at It is my bona fide intention to renounce forever all allegiance and fidelity to any foreign prince, potentate, state, or sovereignty, and particularly to Victor Emmanuel III, King of Italy, of which I am now a subject : I arrived at the port of New York, in the State of New York on or about the 1st day of August, anno Domini 1913 : I am not an anarchist; I am not a polygamist nor a believer in the practice of polygamy; and it is my intention in good faith to become a citizen of the United States of America and to permanently reside therein: SO HELP ME GOD.

Filippo Antonio Dicco
(Original signature of declarant.)

Subscribed and sworn to affirmed before me this 19th day of October, anno Domini 1927

Wirth Gadbury
Clerk of the Circuit Court.

By .... Clerk.

[SEAL.]

11—2203

Declaration of intention Filippo Di-Cicco. These are family members of Don Chick, Patty Brown and Barbara Elwood.

Maria & Filippo Alien Registration

Naturalization certificate of Aristati De Beneditto. He became a citizen in 1908 in East St. Louis, Illinois but later came to Blackford County. Mr. De Beneditto was the grandfather of Bob, Max, and Jackie Tarter.

Many Italians were drawn to Hartford City by the huge glass factories. Some came to this part of Indiana as laborers building and repairing the railroad lines and stayed to work in the glass factories. They were mostly unskilled but willing and able to learn and do whatever job was necessary.

Some must have thought America was a good country and promptly filed naturalization papers. Cornelius Pax celebrated his newly-acquired citizenship a little too riotously. Pax, whose name in Italian meant "peace," acquired a load of "tanglefoot," went to the home of Constable Harve Mullins and proceeded to raise cain. He threw chairs off the porch and frightened the family including Harve almost to death. As a result Cornelius was arrested and fored to pay a fine. It's great to be a new citizen of America. (Daily Times Gazette, July 29, 1908)

Mid 1914 and it seemed that Europe would be plunged into war at any moment. The foreign workmen in Blackford County were anxiously scanning the news and wondering if it would be necessary for them to give up their work here and return to their native countries for army duty. During the recent war between Italy and Turkey, Italian workmen were forced to return home and take up arms. This happened again again during the Balkan War.

European governments were very strict in respect to the military service of their subjects. In case a man refused to respect the call, he would immediately be arrested and imprisoned if he ever returned to his native country. There were probably very few workmen who returned through a feeling of real patriotism to face a general war.

But the Italians and others began to leave. In January 1915 sixteen departed for the purpose of taking their place in the ranks of Italy's armies. Most of the Italians of the county left, going from Hartford City to Pittsburg, then to New York where they were joined by hundreds from all parts of the United States and then on to Italy.

The Italian government sent money to Blackford County to defray the expense of the trip home for its citizens.

An interesting editorial comment in the Evening News appeared on January 16, 1915:

One noticeable thing about the apparent feelings of the Italians who left here was the lack of merriment among them. At the time the Italians were called home about two years before to serve in the Balkan War, the men who left the city seemed to feel that they were leaving for a frolic. Now in 1915 it seemed to be a different matter, for they doubtless realized that the present war was anything but a frolic. And again, the recent earthquake disaster, which laid waste to so much of Italy, probably had its effect upon the feelings of the countrymen here.

Evening News   July 14, 1902

A COLONY OF DAGOES

Few people who reside in this city, in the center of the highest civilized country on the globe, know that a view of Europe on a small scale, the form of an Italian colony may be seen west of the city. Such is the case. Eleven box cars are equipped with all the furnishings of small houses and in them are several adult Italians, besides a large number of women and children.

These Italians, or dagoes, as they are commonly called, have been living in their box car homes for the past three or four months, cooking, eating, sleeping, troubling no one, and expecting no one to trouble them. They have appointed certain ones to do the buying so that a majority of them have never been in this city.

One of the cars is devoted to the laundrying of the clothing of the inhabitants. While to look at the men and women one would think the clothing had never been near the laundry, still when one visits the spot and sees the line of clothing hung up to dry they see that at least a few of them try to keep clean.

The men and boys who are old enough work on the grade and earn fair wages. They have a sort of a pool in which they put some of their money and beer is purchased for the entire force. Checks are then issued to the different members of the colony, so that every man gets his share of the drinks. The bar is one the cars, and has somewhat the appearance of a saloon, although the furnishings are very crude. The game of cards seems to be the favorite game with both old and young and a visitor at the colony is not slow in finding this to be true.

The food is cooked up by different members of the party. Those wishing a meal go to the cook and purchase whatever they want, pay for it and take it to the dining car, where the meals are eaten together. The chief food is macaroni, beans, black coffee and bread. The inhabitants are remarkably healthy and appear to be contented. Now and then the stiletto is unsheated and pandemonium reigns for a time, but as a rule there is peace and quietude.

Evening News   December 16, 1907

HOMESICK DAGO MISSES FRIENDS AT MONTPELIER

A straggling Italian, who had been instructed to join his friends there, but was delayed for some reason in making the trip from the home country, reached Montpelier Friday, according to the <u>Herald</u>, of that city, and was very much disappointed to learn that the gang he expected to find there working on the pipeline for the Ohio Oil Company, had moved on.

A stranger among strangers, and not able to speak or understand one word of our language, he was heart broken and knew not which way to go or what to do. Finally he was turned over to Harry Alexander, who speaks his language, and after learning from him his troubles, Alexander took him to the office of the Indiana Pipeline Company, where he explained to the boys the plight of the stranger and he was given a letter to present to the ticket agents and train men which would land him with his friends who are now working on a line in Ohio.

When asked if he had money with which to buy tickets, he eyed the crowd rather suspiciously, but on being assured by Alexander that they were his friends, he produced a belt that was quite well supplied wit sheckels, and Alexander took him to the station of L. E. & W. and saw to purchasing his ticket and starting him off in a happier frame of mind.

He was a big husky fellow, but when in the course of questions put to him, Tug Wilson suggested that he be asked if he was homesick and wanted to go home, he cried like a broken-hearted child and big salty tears stood in the eyes of all his hearers as they thought of his anguish and what it would mean to them to be placed in a similar position.

Evening News   July 29, 1914

SOUTH SIDE WORKMAN MAY HAVE TO
RETURN IN CASE WAR RESULTS

In case Europe is plunged into war, which at the present moment looks likely, there will probably be a number of foreign workmen at the South

Side factory who will find it necessary to lay down their work here and return to the armies of their native countries.

There are a number of Austrians employed in this city. Greeks also work at the factory, and Italians. During the recent war between Italy and Turkey, Italian workmen from this city were forced to go back home to take up arms. This happened again during the Balkan War.

The European governments are very strict on their subjects with respect to war service. In case a subject refuses to go back when called, he lays himself open to arrest in case he ever returns to his country. There are probably few workmen here who would return through any feeling of patriotism to face a general war.

Evening News   March 15, 1915

ITALIANS ARE TO DEPART SOON

Three With Unpronounceable Names Plan to Leave Hartford City

The closing of the big tank of the American Window Glass factory in March, 1915 caused a number of the Italian workmen employed there to return to their native land.

Lettimo Donatelli, Settimio Brozzi and Giocomo Andonini left for Macchinvaiportore, Italy (Unless you're able to speak more than English you'd better not tell your friends about this). Most of the Italians who had been working in the city were said to come from Macci. etc., and vicinity.

Whether the foreigners felt that America was going on the "bum" or whether they wanted to get back home to fight the Turks was not known. Shortly after the recent earthquake, many Italians left this city for their native land. A number of Bulgarians left during early 1915. Now the foreign population on the South Side was considerably smaller than previously.

Evening News   May 24, 1915

Residents of the South Side reported a brutal assault by American boys on Charles Marcella, an Italian boy. As a result the fellow got two black eyes. According to one resident, the boy was beaten by Zeke Tarr.

The Italian boy worked for Mrs. Prevot who was blind, and the other boys, it was said, were jealous of him because the French lady had taken a fancy to young Marcella.

For more than thirty five years, Mrs. Flora Prevot owned and operated a grocery on South Jefferson Street. She continued in the operation of the grocery business even after she became blind, but was later forced to retire due to ill health.

Undoubtedly, a willing young helper, such as Charles Marcella, would have been of great assistance and comfort to Mrs. Prevot in managing her business, and she in turn rewarded him generously, arousing the ire of his peers. Marcella may have been given police protection to prevent further attacks by ruffians.

Evening News   May 25, 1915

Employees at the railroad station are authority for the statement that thus far since the entrance of Italy into the great European conflict, there have been no Italians leaving this city for their native land.

This is probably due to the fact that most of the Italians who had any idea of returning to Italy did so some time ago. When the Italian army first began preparations for entering the war, there were a number of foreigners who left the city. Some of the residents of the Italian colony on the South Side said that America is good enough for them and that they have no intention of returning across the water to fight. Those who did go back some time ago went back because they had families in the old country.

Evening News   January 16, 1915

DO NOT DESIRE TO RETURN HOME

The departure of Italian residents from Hartford City, for the purpose of taking their places in the ranks of the Peninsular Kingdom's armies, is still going on. It is likely few more will leave here, however, for most the Italian residents who are eligible to call have now left.

Eight foreigners left Tuesday evening and eight more went Wednesday. They go from this city to Pittsburg, where they will be joined by hundreds of other Italians from all part of the United States. From Pittsburg the Italians are sent to New York City and thence to Italy.

One noticeable thing about the apparent feelings of the Italians who leave here is the lack of merriment among them. At the time the Italians were called home, about two years ago, for the Balkan war, the men who left the city seemed to feel that they were leaving for a frolic. Now it seems to be a different matter, for they doubtless realize that the present war is anything but a frolic. And again, the recent earthquake disaster, which laid waste to so much of Italy, probably has its effect upon the feelings of the countrymen here.

The Italian government has been sending money to this city for its citizens, to defray the expense of the trip home. The Italians do not dare refuse to go, else they would never dare return to their native land in the future.

Evening News   August 3, 1914

It is true that people do not always live together in peace and harmony, and thus it was with the Italians on the South Side.

According to the story told by the Italians, Frank Buonsignoce, Drazzio Cappablanca and Tony Durand, they spent Saturday evening at the home of Mike Ropon, Italian boss at the South Side factory, who lived on South Spring Street. They had not been drinking. On their way home they met four Americans near the Diamond Saloon at the corner of Monroe and Fifth Streets. The strangers had some trouble with a number of Frenchmen and then six or seven shots rang out.

The first shot hit Buonsignoce in his left eye, then went downward lodging in his neck. At first it was thought the shot was fatal. The injured man was taken to Fort Wayne and every effort was made to save his eyesight.

It was believed that the assailant boarded the last southbound interurban car and headed for Muncie. A few days later it was announced that Buonsignoce would not lose the sight in his eye. He also stated that he did not know who did the shooting.

These were rough times! The police always had to be alert on the South Side.

Evening News   November 15, 1915

RESIST OFFICER ON WAY TO JAIL

The Southside Italian colony furnished police court proceedings for Sunday afternoon and Monday, three of the law violators being from the recently returned foreign element which has come to work at the plant of the American Window Glass factory.

Two of the men, giving their names as Frank Logi, of 1606 South Monroe Street, and Vitturious Pernaggle, were taken up early Saturday night, charged with intoxication.

After being started to jail the two turned upon Marshal Pursley, who had made the arrest, declaring they would kill him. Near the jail, the two dagoes put up a desperate fight, but were subdued by the officer, assisted by a passerby.

The men were tried at 2 o'clock Sunday afternoon before Mayor E. W. Secrest. Both men at that time denied that they had made any attempts to get away. They claimed that they had had beer at the home of Logi which had been ordered through a local agency and that Pernaggle had brought whiskey with him from Lima, Ohio, Saturday.

The foreigners were given fines of $1 and costs each, which Logi immediately paid.

Monday morning Jack Chick, a foreigner, who with his wife operates a rooming and boarding house on the Southside, complained to the police that a man by the name of Tony Darand had beat him out of a bill for storage of his goods. The matter was investigated and Darand was arrested and arraigned before Mayor Secrest at the jail. The foreigner was given a fine of $1 and costs for beating a board bill which he also owed, and was forced to make arrangements to pay the bill to Chick. The fine was paid.

Some trouble is expected by the police from the Italian element of the Southside this winter. A special policeman for that part of the city may be appointed.

In the year following the end of World War I, a new law was enacted allowing ex-soldiers who were not citizens of the United States to become naturalized without going through as much red tape as ordinary persons. The law provided that an ex-soldier could become a naturalized citizen by presenting an honorable discharge and by proving by two witnesses that he was the man to whom the papers had been issued.

The first man to take advantage of the new law was a Greek, the second was Drazzio Cappablanca, an employee of the American Window Glass. Their petitions were filed the first week in October, 1919. Cappablanca's discharge papers showed he had served in Company B, 347th M. G. Ba. Mike Ropon and Cloyd Runk appeared as his witnesses. Cappablana came to this country in 1911.

Mike Ropon was a well-known Italian resident of Hartford City who lived at 522 East Main Street. Mike Ropon worked at the American Window Glass Company for 27 years as head of the producer gas department. He was a dependable workman, a good citizen, and the most prominently known Italian in the city.

Hartford City Times Gazette   September 10, 1927

DEATH TAKES MIKE ROPON

Mike Ropon was a prominently-known Italian resident of the community and had a great many friends.

Mr. Ropon would have been 49 on September 28. He was born in Italy, but had been a resident of America for many years. In 1900 at Jeanette, Pennsylvania, he claimed Miss Madeline Pucinna as his bride. She died on October 8 last.

A brother, Joe, lives in Pennsylvania. The whereabouts of Mr. Ropon's sisters, who also came to America, are not known.

Mr. Ropon had five children, who are Mrs. Francis Pouder, of Muncie; Lewis Ropon, of Long Beach, California; Miss Thelma, George, and James Ropon, of this city.

He was a member of St. John's Catholic Church.

Times Gazette   October 27, 1927

Pasquale Paolo, who has been in the county jail since the night of October 15, when he shot and killed Frank Stone, probably will be released Thursday.

It seems likely that no charges will be lodged against Paolo following the report of the grand jury, which held that evidence in the case did not warrant a charge. The grand jury held that Paolo shot Stone in self defense.

ITALIANS APPLYING FOR CITIZENSHIP IN BLACKFORD COUNTY

Name	Date of Arrival
Bornia, Salvatore	June 9, 1908
Bovina, Salvatore	April 6, 1908
Bovino, Pasquale	July 22, 1908
Brusa, John	July 8, 1901
Caladrella, Antonio	March 21, 1908
Calogero, Lipira	April 14, 1906
Campis, Giuseppe	March 28, 1908
Cappabianca, Orazio	April 12, 1911
Caputo, Domenico	April 21, 1907
Caputo, James	January 28, 1901
Cardela, Vincenzo	March 27, 1906
Carozza, Giuseppe	June 13, 1913
Chick, Frank	April 23, 1907
Chick, Jack	October 24, 1910
Cicoro, Antonio	September 6, 1913
Colangelo, Antonio	February 15, 1908
Coletta, Giovanni	March 10, 1904
Cunecolo, Antonio	June 4, 1900
Cusano, Angelo	May 11, 1906
Dagastino, Michelle	January 7, 1921
DeAgostino, Antonio	December 27, 1920
DeCicco, Gioachino	October 24, 1910
DePalma, Louis	March 29, 1909
DiCicco, Antonio	August 1, 1913
DiFrancesco, Mariano	May 11, 1907
DiMattoo, Rocco	March 24, 1902
Donatelli, John	September 2, 1913
Durante, Antonio	June 7, 1912
Framichele, Mariano	February 7, 1906
Fuses, Salvatore	April 9, 1908
Giacomo, Smeriglia	March 25, 1908
Gronati, Savirio	April 26, 1905
James, Tom	October 27, 1907
Lacerna, Joseph	May 20, 1908
Lapenta, Giuseppe	March 28, 1908
Maffei, Antonio	April 18, 1905
Menichello, Grochino	March 15, 1906

Mercurio, Joseph	April 22, 1908
Messines, Leonard	October 10, 1908
Mortise, Orazio	April 6, 1908
Nizzardi, Giuseppe	June 1, 1912
Pack, Cornellus	March 8, 1901
Pagano, Francesco	March 1, 1908
Palara, Salvatore	March 23, 1900
Paone, Joseph	March 24, 1908
Peluso, Donato	November 4, 1908
Permazza, Vittorio	August 21, 1907
Pruzire, Remizei	April 5, 1908
Puzella, Bartolmen	April 17, 1906
Puzella, Raffaella	February 10, 1902
Puzello, Giovanbattesta	May 10, 1908
Rapuano, Giuseppe	May 18, 1902
Ropnono, Joseph	May 30, 1902
Ropuono, Michelle	April 22, 1891
Ruggeri, Francesco	December 16, 1907
Sabatino, Giuseppe	November 18, 1906
Sanchella, Frank	March 15, 1906
Scavina, Giuseppe	April 6, 1908
Scuena, Francesco	April 6, 1908
Sescio, Tony	August 1, 1913
Smeriglia, Giacomo	March 25, 1908

THE POLISH

A 1916 advertisement for Stein's Clothing Store in Hartford City.

A 1937 advertisement showcasing Mr. Stein's celebration of 20 years in business on the north side of the square.

Interior of Stein's Clothing Store, later located at 115 West Washington Street.

Evening News   August 3, 1915

CANNOT AID HIS FAMILY

Vincent Sebnevskey, a Pole, living on the South Side, is a downhearted man, for with his wife and children in the state of Warsaw, near the city of that name, where some of the heaviest fighting of the European war has been in progress for weeks, he is unable to get assistance to them.

The foreigner sent some money to his relatives, amounting to approximately $50. Recently he received notice that the money could not be delivered and that he could regain it by calling at the post office. He had attempted to send it by means of a post office money order.

Sebnevskey fears that his loved ones have come to grief since the outbreak of the struggle. He is also out of a job and is all around, "up against it." There is no use for him to attempt further communication with his wife at this time and as a result can do nothing but await developments.

Daily Times Gazette   June 28, 1921

Hersh Etstein of Montpelier filed his declaration of intention to become a citizen of the U. S. in the county clerk's office. He came to this country from Ludwipol, Poland in April of this year. Mr. Etstein is a tailor by trade and has a brother in the clothing business at Montpelier.

SEYMOUR STEIN

Seymour Stein was born in Tutchin, Poland, the son of Samuel Stein. The senior Mr. Stein was in the drygoods business in the same location for 66 years until his death in 1938. He was a successful and widely known business man. Thus the son Seymour had learned as a child from an expert

145

the purchase and resale of clothing and the management of a clothing store.

The Stein Clothing Store was first established in Montpelier about 1922 or 1923. Then in 1925 it was moved to Hartford City into a building on the south side of the public square. In time the store occupied places west of Gough's Drug Store, briefly on the north side of the square, and finally in the Kirshbaum building at the southwest corner of the square. Mr. Stein based his success on the high grade of merchandise sold in the store and the courteous treatment and geniality received by the customers.

Clyde White was a long-time clerk and assistant manager. Other employees were Louis Guignard and Chris Zenz.

Dealie (Mrs. Ron) Dodds, member of the Blackford County Historical Society, remembers that she and her sister worked in the store during their high school years and that Mr. Stein was a dapper little man, astute in business, always friendly with his customers. Mr. Stein taught her to shorten men's shirt sleeves by taking the sleeve out at the shoulder instead of taking off the cuff. When she protested at shortening men's dress suit coats, he assured that, "You can do it." And she did.

Mr. and Mrs. Stein were parents of two sons, Laurel, known familiarly as Dick, and Marshall. Both boys were handsome, outstanding in school and well respected by their peers. But tragedy struck when Marshall, during his senior year in high school, was diagnosed with Hodgkin's disease. This rare illness affects the glands of the body, and science had discovered no cure. Specialists at John Hopkins, the Cleveland Clinic, the Duke Clinic and elsewhere were consulted, but none knew of anything effective.

Marshall was able to attend the Hartford City-Peru basketball game on Friday and took a number of pictures for the Retro, the high school yearbook. Photography was one of his hobbies as well as reading. His death occurred early Sunday morning December 10, 1939.

Mr. Stein successfully ran Stein's Clothing store for more than 34 years until 1957 when he retired and sold the store to Richard's of Marion. The store, located at the southwest corner of the public square, continued in business for several more years.

In August 1959 Mr. and Mrs. Stein sold their home at 516 East Main Street to Mr. and Mrs. Sam Boswell who came to Hartford City from Hobart, Indiana. Mr. Boswell was associated with the Rural Loan and Savings Association. Mr. and Mrs. Stein held an auction of their household furnishings preliminary to leaving Hartford City. They went for a time to Columbus, Ohio, where their son Dick resided, and then to Florida where they made their permanent home.

POLISH APPLYING FOR CITIZENSHIP
IN BLACKFORD COUNTY

Name	Date of Arrival
Crodbock, John	March 14, 1899
Damarick, John	March 18, 1901
Dominick, George	April 25, 1902
Elsztejn, Sura	April 5, 1921
Epstein, Harry	April 7, 1921
Etstein, Hersh	April 7, 1921
Etstein, Sarah	April 5, 1907
Hatzyn, Ed	March 10, 1905
Kalzny, Adam	May 13, 1905
Prataicsyk, Walck	April 25, 1902
Vincent, Fred	May, 1912

THE ROUMANIANS

August, 1901, photo showing group of laborers working on grade work for railroad

October 26, 1903

EVENED UP ON THE POOR COOK

Two Roumanians who herd with a gang of compatriots in the Roumanian settlement in the rear of the National Rolling Mill went to Muncie yesterday and returned with their systems well saturated with corn juice. Thoughts of tough grub inflicted on them for many days at their boarding house rankled in their brains along with the seething liquor and they evened up on the cook. The cook fought as well as he could but he was soon put out of commission. The marshal went to the boarding house at the request of a young Roumanian, but he found nobody there but the cook with a battered head and a throat sore from choking. He said his assailants had fled to the woods, but he promised to file affidavits today.

Daily Times Gazette   July 31, 1908

Jacob Pitzinsky, a Roumanian employed in the cellar at the South Side factory, had the base of his thumb cut severely last night.

ROMANIANS APPLYING FOR CITIZENSHIP IN BLACKFORD COUNTY

Name	Date of Arrival
Bogle, Pete	March 13, 1900
Bunch, San	October 15, 1900
Fleisher, Nic	May 9, 1900
Fleisher, Zak	May 9, 1900
German, Nic	May 9, 1902
Hoffner, John	September 5, 1900
Killaman, Nic	November 15, 1900
Maetra, Mike	June 15, 1900
Monzar, Zac	May 9, 1901
Mozawu, Nick	February 12, 1901
Pete, Joe	November 10, 1900
Pete, John	January 1, 1902

THE RUSSIANS

Howard Smilack was the son of El Smilack. The picture was taken in front of the Smilack home at 306 East Main Street. Howard is shown here with his bicycle and pony, Bluebird.

Mr. and Mrs. El Smilack

City Dir. 1902

E. SMILACK

DEALER IN

Scrap Iron and Metals,
Rags,
Gas and Oil Well Rope,
Hides,
Pelts,
Furs,
Tallow,
Beeswax,
Cracklings and Tankage.

PHONE 370.
HARTFORD CITY, INDIANA.

White House,

Near Business Center.

Rates $1.00 a Day.

Special Rates
by the Week.

Not only a place to board but a place where one can enjoy all the comforts of home life.

MRS. J. D. WHITE,
PROPRIETOR.

302 E. Water St.. HARTFORD CITY.

The Time Is Here

The time is here to do your butchering and trapping furs. Don't look for Wild Cat Markets, There is a market at

El Smilack's

In your home city.

Highest prices for hides, furs and tallow.

Also handle coal and wood, and buy all kinds of junk.

Phones -- Office 370.   Yard 238·   Residence 634.

Advertisements for Smilack business.

E.Smilack
205 EAST WASH.
Phone 370   Hartford City

SECOND HAND PIPE
AND OLD OIL
WELLS, ETC.

COAL AND WOOD

E. Smilack
205 East Wash.   Phone 370
Hartford City, Ind.

E.Smilack Wholesale Dealer in Scrap
205 EAST WASH.   Iron, metals, hides fur, wool
Hartford City.   & second hand pipe & oil well supplies

Advertisements for Smilack business.

Band in parade on 200 block of East Washington Street in front
of Mr. Smilack's store. The photo was taken in 1906.

<u>The Daily Gazette</u>   August 4, 1902

SMILACK BUYS BUSINESS SITE

El Smilack, the East Washington Street junk merchant, closed a deal Monday for the 40 feet west of the Peter Maddox livery barn on East Washington Street. The consideration was $2000.

It is the intention of Mr. Smilack to erect a two-story brick block on the site at once where he will continue in the junk business. The lower floor will consist of but one room and afford ample room for the expansion of his rapidly growing business.

Smilack is a native of Russia and came to this city about seven years ago. Handicapped by being unacquainted with the ways and customs of American people and unable to speak the English language he set to work to make a living. He began buying junk and by clever business tactics has accumulated considerable wealth. He has many friends in the city who are pleased to know that he is prospering.

<u>Evening News</u>   December 19, 1905

HE GREW TIRED OF THE SERVICE

A Soldier of the Czar Has Arrived Here To Join Relatives

Another soldier of the czar has arrived in Hartford City. He is Herman Smilack, a cousin of El Smilack, and a brother of Fred Smilack, who, in company with Isadore Schuler, recently arrived on these shores from Russia.

Herman Smilack, until a few weeks ago, was in the service of his emperor at St. Petersburg. An order came for the transfer of his regiment to Manchuria to fight the Japanese, and Herman, not liking the outlook, severed his connection with the army. Being a private, he was not in a position to offer his resignation, and he left without saying a word. He does not like to be called a deserter, but that's what he is in the Russian language. He made his way to Bremen, Germany, and took passage for God's country. Such was his haste that he did not have time to change his uniform for citizens' clothes, and he arrived here in the livery of the autocrat of all the Russias, somewhat the worse for wear, but still buoyant and happy to have escaped from service that became distasteful with the prospect of a cheerless campaign in the far east.

Young Smilack joined the Russian army—not from choice, however—at the age of 21. He served two years and he still owes four years of service to the czar—six years being the time every able-bodied citizen of Russia must serve, in theory, at least, in the army. In spite of his desertion, Smilack is intensely Russian in feeling and he declares that his country will win the war with Japan. He declares Russia has so many men at its command that it is only a matter of time when numbers will prevail against the limited resources of Japan. Regiment after regiment is now going to the front.

The newcomer from Russia is a typical soldier in appearance—straight as an arrow, alert and vigorous. He wears a moustache trained to points and tilted after the manner Kaiser Bill of Germany. One can imagine that an army of such men would battle desperately and one wonders what sort of soldiers the Japanese can be to put up such a brave fight against them.

Telegram   July 5, 1906

Maxim Smilack, a brother of E. Smilack, the East Washington Street junk dealer, arrived in the city from his home in Russia. He is 22 years of age and is a butcher by trade, but will most likely engage in the junk business in some surrounding town. July 5 was the first meeting of the brothers in 12 years. The trip for Maxim to this city from his home in Russia was a long one, as he was on the way 5 weeks. Some misunderstanding in regard to his ticket caused him to be delayed nearly two weeks and the trip on the whole was a very tiresome one. He was accompanied by four relatives who stopped at Dunkirk where they will make their future home, two relatives being in the junk business at that place.

<u>Telegram</u> September 19, 1906

LETTER FROM LAND OF CZAR

El Smilack has received a letter from his father in Russia which makes the son apprehensive for the father's safety. The elder Smilack lives 80 miles away from Smolensk, which has been one of the centers of the frightful massacres which have disgraced the Russian nation, and the depredations are extending to the Smilack neighborhood.

The elder Smilack was formerly engaged in the practice of law, but now, at the age of 60, he is living on a farm. His letter gives the details of the massacres. In Russia the sale of intoxicating liquors is monopolized by the government. In every center there is a large government building devoted to the sale of intoxicants and this monopoly is more or less responsible for the excesses of the soldiery. Nearly every massacre of Jews in Russia has been preceded by a raid on the part of the soldiers upon government liquor headquarters. After drinking their fill of vodka the soldiers not infrequently destroy the warehouse and then sally forth to take pot shots at the Jews they meet.

Mr. Smilack writes from Russia that up to the disbandment of the douma he felt safe from a visit from the czar's assassins. Now, however, the field of rapine and murder is spreading, and Mr. Smilack fears that in time his place will be visited and the worst may happen.

El Smilack has written to his father to hasten to "Free America" even if he has to sacrifice all he has to do so. El has a sister at Toledo, Ohio and a brother in this city. The brothers offer to contribute to their father's support if he will come to this country to live and they think he would be satisfied to live with the sister at Toledo, because there are many Russians there.

<u>Evening News</u> February 27, 1908

RUSSIAN WALKS ALL THE WAY FROM BIRMINGHAM

Timothy Karavan, a native of far-away Russia, is a new attaché of the El Smilack establishment on East Washington street.

Karavan took up his abode in Hartford City in an unusual manner. Two years ago he sailed to America from his native land and took employment in a steel mill in Alabama. With arrival of the financial depression, the Alabama mill discontinued operation. Karavan had but $17 when he took his departure northward, and after weeks of traveling on foot he finally reached Columbus, Ohio. His funds were exhausted when he left Columbus west bound, walking along the railway tracks on foot. After traveling nearly four days without food, he reached Hartford City. He is unable to speak English and his difficulties as he traveled may be imagined.

In El Smilack, who is Russian by birth, Karavan found a friend. El has given the foreigner employment in his shop. However, El says Karavan is cut out for a farmer and will probably take a job as a farm hand later.

Daily Times Gazette   January 4, 1921

MONTPELIER RUSSIAN HEARS FROM FAMILY

Max Plank, a junk dealer at Montpelier, received a letter from his wife living in Russia, the first word from her in four years. His wife and four children live at Astrakan on the Caspian Sea. She reports that, while they have seen little actual fighting in their section of Russia, they have suffered from economic conditions and have been barely able to keep alive. The oldest son, 16, is able to earn the equal of only 16 cents a day in American money.

Mr. Plank endeavored about four years ago to send for his family, but the New York firm, acting as his agent in forwarding tickets, tried in vain to get into communication with the family, and returned Mr. Plank's money to him. He has received his first naturalization papers and will dispatch tickets for his family to join him as soon as he gets his final citizenship papers.

Hartford City Times Gazette   October 9, 1922

Mrs. Plavonik and Children Arrive Monday

The little Pennsylvania station here was the scene of a touching reunion at 3:45 o'clock this morning when Mendel Plavonick, better known as Max Plank, Russian junk dealer of Montpelier, greeted his wife and four children, who had arrived on the 1:49 train from the east.

The train was late, arriving here about 2:15. Plank had expected the family to come by way of Fort Wayne, some time today or tonight. Therefore he was not at the station to greet them.

The mother and four children got off the train and appealed to Charles

Stump, employee of the Pennsylvania. They could speak no English and Stump had difficulty in finding out who they were.

Finally Stump was able to make out the word "Montpelier" in their conversation. It then occurred to him it might be Plank's family. He mentioned the name Plank or Plavonik, writing it down. The mother recognized the word and nodded her head. She then produced papers with Plank's name written upon them.

Plank was called at once at Montpelier. He was surprised, though delighted, that his family had arrived so soon from New York, and came here at once in a touring car to get them.

Incidents of great importance in the lives of people often are the simplest. It was so in the greeting between the Russian and his family. The husband and wife embraced each other fondly, but not so long. The younger children seemed a little backward, for they did not recognize their father, as it had been 10 years since they had seen him. The older children knew him, however. The older boy, 19 years of age, had talked with his father over the telephone when Plank was first located at Montpelier, shortly after their arrival.

Plank took the members of the family to Montpelier at once. He has a home prepared for them there. The four children seem to be in excellent condition physically. They were well and comfortably dressed. The mother, who is 38 years of age, looked more like a woman of 50. She shows the effects of the hardships through which she has passed during the past eight years.

The family arrived in New York last Friday aboard the liner Carmania. They were detained for a time at Ellis Island. The mother was worried during that time, fearing there would be some angle develop which would cause them to be turned back into the clutches of the soviet. They were not detained in New York long, however.

Rachel, aged 12, is the youngest of the children, while Sarah, aged 16 is the second girl. The two girls, together with Boris, a lad of 14 years, had no recollection of their father. Aaron, the oldest boy, had only an indistinct memory of the father.

The children apparently are strong and healthy. The difference in the appearance of the mother and her flock suggests that the mother must have denied herself food many times so there would be enough of their sparse rations for the mouths of her children.

"I'm just half myself," was the way Mrs. Plavonik spoke of her decrease in weight due to hard work, worry, and undernourishment. However, she has gained since the American relief commission reached her with food packages and she should be strong again. The fact that the mother and children know only two words of English—those two words being "America" and "Indiana"—made an interview difficult although two or three interpreters helped with the questions and answers at the port of New York. The youngest child added two new words to her English vocabulary when she said "thank you" for candy.

The children, though they could not make themselves understood with the spoken word, grinned with happiness.

"No good," was the children's description of Russia in answering a question put by a freckle-faced Jewish lad who acted as interpreter.

The children were in rags and tatters while in Russia, but they arrived here well clothed by the American relief commission, which expended funds advanced by the father. The shoes and clothes they wear cost many million rubles. Rather than having the appearance of children who lived so long in poverty, they looked like they were all dressed up for Sunday school.

Rather than be interviewed about themselves, they questioned. They asked curious questions about the father whom they didn't remember. The boy was told that the father, to simplify his Russian name, is known at Montpelier as Mr. Plank.

In order to conserve the limited means of the father and husband, the family came over third class.

"It's all like a dream—can it be possible that we are at last in America?" exclaimed the little mother, turning to the interpreter. A smile enveloped her face for a moment and then she breathed a deep sigh, her smile giving way to a worried look. Still held on the boat she feared something would yet happen to cause her to be turned back.

While her husband's naturalization as an American automatically made her and the two younger children American citizens, the two older children, being more than 16, were regarded as Russians until they had actually stepped on American soil, and for this reason, were treated as ordinary aliens and had to have their admittance formally passed on by the Ellis Island authorities.

It was last April, soon after the husband and father was naturalized, that he began an effort to obtain the family's release from Russia and their departure from Russia. The American state department, working through unofficial channels because of no diplomatic relations with soviet Russia, exerted its best efforts to obtain the family's release, but so many obstacles had to be overcome it was only a month ago that the way was opened for them to come to America.

The father, spending his surplus cash to obtain the family's passage and to prepare for their home, was unable to go to New York to receive them.

Several of Mrs. Plavonik's relatives died during the war and since. It is regarded as remarkable that she was able to keep her family together.

Plank came to America about two years before the European war broke out. He meant to bring his family after him as soon as possible. Before he could do this, however, the European war had broken out and he could not bring his people here.

<u>Hartford City Times Gazette</u>   July 14, 1922

The remains of the five crossing accident victims who were killed Thursday afternoon when the automobile in which they were riding, was struck by a west bound Pennsylvania passenger train, No. 811, will be taken to Cleveland, Ohio for burial.

The dead are El Smilack, 49, wealthy business man of this city; his two daughters, Sophia, 13, and Celia, 14; Mrs. Julius Karklin, 46, and her son, Robert, age 7, of Cleveland, Ohio. The injured are are: Mrs. El Smilack; Mrs. Sam Levi, daughter of Mrs. Karklin, and Howard Smilack, age 7.

<u>Hartford City Times Gazette</u>   July 14, 1922

El Smilack's Life Was Very Unusual One

History of His Life Is Most Interesting—He Spoke Several Languages

El Smilack's rise in the business world was a clear example of what hard work and honest business dealing will do in an atmosphere like that of America, where a man has a chance to advance.

Mr. Smilack was penniless when he came to Hartford City. He drove here from Marion with one horse and a wagon and went into the junk business in East Washington Street. His first establishment was located at the corner of Washington and Monroe Streets in a tumble down frame building.

By dint of hard work and honest dealings he gradually got ahead in the world until, at the time of his death, he leaves his wife and son with a comfortable fortune.

Mr. Smilack had had a very interesting life. Born in the province of Smolensk, Russia, under the old regime of the czars, he had seen service in the Russian army before he came to America. At one time he was a guard in the Siberian prison camp. Dissatisfied with conditions in Russia and recognizing the cruelty and oppression which ruled it, Mr. Smilack escaped from the Russian army and came to America.

With coming of prosperity to him in his adopted land, Mr. Smilack did not forget his relatives in his native land. For years he sent money to his father, Antrim Smilack, and continued to assist his parents until conditions in Russia became so bad that it was impossible to get help to his people any longer. During the famine period in Russia both his father and mother perished to the great sorrow of the son.

A sister lives in the province of Smolensk. Mr. Smilack of late months has made repeated efforts to send money and sustenance to her without success. It will be weeks before she will learn of her brother's sudden and untimely death.

Besides his junk, coal and wood business, Mr. Smilack had in the later years of his life engaged in the oil business in this and other states. He owned the building in which his business was located, also a farm of 124 acres in Jay County. He carried life insurance running well up into six figures.

Eighteen years ago Mr. Smilack claimed Miss Gertrude Ruben, then a resident of Muncie, as his wife. Since coming to this city, his estimable wife has won the highest regard of all who know her.

The two daughters, Celia, 14, and Sophia, 13, and the son who were born at the Smilack home at 306 East Main Street had always lived in this city. The children attended the public schools and were favorites among their friends and playmates. Mr. Smilack and his wife spared no effort in their family's behalf, and his children had become talented musicians.

Mr. Smilack had received a good education in his native land. As a business man he was foresquare, and upright in every matter and his honesty was undoubted. He foresight and business judgment were remarkably good. In his varied experience over the world he had learned to speak several foreign languages fluently.

Although he himself, immediately upon coming to America, became an American in the true sense of the word and was ever bent upon acquiring a better understanding of the English language and of American customs, El Smilack was ever ready to help those of his race here. Recently he had done much to assist Mac Plavonik, Montpelier Russian, who is attempting to bring his family here from Russia. Mr. Smilack himself tutored Plavonik in the American Constitution, in order that the latter could pass final examination for American citizenship. It was he who was first to grasp Plavonik's hand in congratulations when the court granted the final papers.

In Russia, Mr. Smilack's name was Smilackoff. He was born in Petrovitz in the province of Smolensk, Russia on October 15, 1872. His father Abraham, was an attorney by profession. Mr. Smilack's mother died when he was eighteen months old. He was the youngest of four children. The father married a second time and this wife perished along with him during the Russian famine period. To the second union was born one son who returned to Russia, after coming to America for a time. He returned to Russia just before the outbreak of the World War. One of Mr. Smilack's brothers died young. Another married and remained in Russia and another brother also remained in the old country.

Mr. Smilack, whose first name in full was Elbert, was of a fairly prosperous family, in the old days of Russia. He grew up in his native land and was very well educated there. He learned the trade of a confectioner and after a few years was employed as commercial representative for a loaf sugar manufacturing concern. He was with that house from the age of 16 to the age of 21, being secretary and bookkeeper in the office during the first year and after that time traveling extensively over a large part of the empire. At 21 years of age, Mr. Smilack was pressed into the military service for a period of six years, belonging to the dragoons but after a period of four years and six months was relieved from further duty because of his excellent record.

The News   September 8, 1915

Philip Jasser, 20, and Abraham Weistman, 20, both natives of Beltzi, Russia, and former schoolmates in their native land, took out first papers for naturalization with County Clerk Farrell. They are going to reside in Hartford City and will open an office here for selling goods, canvassing this and surrounding cities.

The two Russians are intelligent looking chaps and speak English remarkably well considering that they have been in America less than two years. Jasser stated that he was born in Beltzi on July 5, 1895 and sailed to this country from Bremen, Germany on the King Albert arriving February 26, 1914. His friend Weistman was born in Beltzi on August 13, 1895 and sailed from Hamburg, Germany on the Graf Vanderzee, arriving here January 25, 1914. They inquired of Clerk Farrell whether it would be necessary for them to take out a license to canvass the city and were informed that they would not provided they were residents of the town.

They asserted their intentions of making Hartford City their permanent residence. They have been in the city about two weeks.

Hartford City Times Gazette   September 12, 1929

I. SUSSMAN IS BACK HOME

Isadore Sussman, local junk dealer who has been spending the past six weeks on a trip to Memel, Lithuania, visiting his mother, three brothers and a sister whom he had not seen since he came to the U. S. 23 years ago, returned home.

Mr. Sussman made the trip on the crack German liner Bremen, which plies between the ports of New York and Bremen.

From the German city of Bremen, he went across north Germany to Lithuania, stopping to visit relatives in Berlin,

Memel is on the border between Germany and Lithuania. Mr. Sussman states the he was wonderfully received by his relatives and was the guest of honor at a big dinner on the day of his arrival. His relatives at first could hardly recognize him. "I had a great time, but I am certainly glad to be back in the old U. S. A., " the Hartford City man remarked.

Hartford City News-Times   August 10, 1940

Isadore Sussman, whose mother is a resident of Lithuania, a small country on the Baltic Sea occupied by Russia, recently received word from her that she and her daughter are safe. Money sent to them by the Hartford City man was received. Just across the street from them is the new Russo-German border.

RUSSIANS APPLYING FOR CITIZENSHIP IN BLACKFORD COUNTY

Name	Date of Arrival	
Boxerman, Samuel	August 1, 1913	
Jasser, Phillip	February 26, 1914	
Michalewitz, Isaac	May 19, 1906	(Lithuania)
Plank, Max	May 24, 1913	
Plavnik, Mandel	May 24, 1913	
Roberts, Michael	March 25, 1906	
Smilack, Elbert	November 2, 1897	
Smilack, Herman	November, 1904	
Sussman, Isador	May 19, 1906	(Lithuania)
Tousencumewnr, Corowonr	November 22, 1907	
Tousencumewnr, Miliona	November 22, 1907	
Tuholski, Stany	March 4, 1906	
Urbanski, Joe	May 4, 1905	
Weitsman, Abraham	January 25, 1914	

THE SWEDISH, NORWEGIANS, AND FINNISH

Olaf Hedstrom relaxing at the lake.

Olaf Hedstrom made a significant contribution to the Hartford City Paper Company with the introduction of glassine or grease-proof paper.

OLAF HEDSTROM

As the originator and developer of an exceedingly important industry at Hartford City, the name of Olaf Hedstrom deserves a high place among Blackford County's industrial leaders. Mr. Hedstom was a man whose concentration of efforts along one line brought about success and prosperity, not only where he is individually concerned, but produced a permanent and increasing benefit to the community. Reared and educated in Sweden, with exceptional training and the influence of a good family behind him, Mr. Hedstrom early took up the paper making business in its technical phases, and after a broad and thorough experience in Europe brought his ideas to America and finally identified himself with the paper mills at Hartford City. He now controls a large interest in that industry, and as the perfecter of certain grades of papers, he has given Blackford County a deserved fame among the paper producing centers of this country.

Olaf Hedstrom was born in Norrkoping, Sweden, October 1, 1875, and his family for generations back had occupied substantial and honored positions in that country. His father, Anders Gustaf Hedstrom, was born in Ostergotland Province, where was born the mother, whose maiden name was Hanna Zetterlund. Throughout his active career the father followed the sea, became master and captain of a coasting vessel, and a few years ago he retired and he and his wife are now living quietly in the town where their son Olaf was born. The father is now ninety years of age, and his wife seventy-six. This veteran sea captain after forty-five years of active service was given a decoration and medal from a Swedish patriotic society as an award for his splendid and efficient care of his crew and of the property of which he had the management and control. He was one of the most careful men who ever sailed the high seas, and possessed all the finer qualities of the seamen. He and his family are members of the State church of Sweden. They were the parents of two sons and four

171

daughters. The son Gustaf, is manager of a woolen mill at Boras, Sweden, is married and has a son and three daughters. The daughter, Thekla, is the wife of Knut Markstrom, and lives in Sweden, and has one daughter. The other married daughter, Hanna, is the wife of Emanuel Axselson, lives in Sweden, and has a son and a daughter. Olaf Hedstrom was reared and educated in his native city, and was graduated with the degree of civil engineer from a technical college with the class of 1894. Two years after leaving college were spent in a paper mill in his native town, and he then went as assistant superintendent to another mill at Klarafors, and was there for seven years. In the meantime he took opportunity to visit Germany and study the mode of making grease proof and glassine papers, which are manufactured in many variegated colors and designs and which were brought to a high state of perfection in the German centers of manufacture. In 1905, Mr. Hedstrom brought the process to the United States, and he deserves the credit for having introduced these special forms of paper manufacture in this country. As an educated man, he was already familiar with the language and the commercial conditions of this country, and the first six months were spent in travel in various states and in study of paper mill conditions. In December, 1905, he found himself in Hartford City, and here formed a satisfactory relationship and was given the opportunity to manufacture his special designs of papers. The Hartford City Paper Company adapted his plans, and as superintendent of those mills they have developed a business which is distinctive and the product has a sale all over the United States. About one hundred and thirty-five people are employed throughout the year in the mills, and this is, of course, one of the largest single items in Hartford City's industrial prosperity. Mr. Hedstrom was married in Hartford City, to Miss Ernestine Johnson, who was born in Ohio, but reared and educated in Hartford City. Her father was a veteran of the Civil War and died some years ago, while her mother is still living in Hartford City, about fifty years of age. Mr. and Mrs. Hedstrom have one son, Olaf Hamilton Hedstrom, born June 24, 1909. Mrs. Hedstrom is a member of the Presbyterian Church, and Mr. Hedstrom has membership in the Blackford Golf Club.

FROM THE <u>HARTFORD CITY NEWS TIMES</u>, SEPTEMBER 6, 1942

Olaf Hedstrom Dies of Heart Attack Friday

After a short period in Canada and in the state of Maine, Mr. Hedstrom came to Hartford City to become superintendent of the Hartford City

Paper Company. He brought with him the process for the manufacture of greaseproof and glassine papers. It was by circumstance that he located here, having seen in a trade journal the announcement that the company here was seeking the services of a specialist in the manufacture of paper. The process was immediately successful in this country and the plant here quickly took its position as a leading paper manufacturing business. Mr. Hedstrom became vice president and general manager of the company in June, 1932, and a year later, following the death of B. A. VanWinkle in June, 1933, became president and general manager. Surviving Mr. Hedstrom are the wife, the son, Lieutenant Hedstrom, the daughter-in-law and granddaughter, one brother, a resident of Stockholm, and three sisters residing at Norrkoping. A man of brilliant mind, Mr. Hedstrom quickly acquired a large vocabulary in the English language. He soon became a citizen of his adopted country and showed by his daily life how completely he endorsed the precepts of freedom and liberty for which both America and his native Sweden stand. For a number of years he served as a member of the board of directors of the Citizen's State Bank. He was a member of the board of trustees of the Presbyterian Church and a member of the Rotary Club and of the Masonic Lodge.

Louise Clamme and Sinuard Castelo

SWEDISH, NORWEGIANS, FINNISH APPLYING FOR CITIZENSHIP IN BLACKFORD COUNTY

Name	Date of Arrival	
Agerspm. Loui	November 11, 1866	(Norway)
Anderson, John	July 12, 1893	(Sweden)
Carrolson, Francis	November 19, 1864	(Finland)
Green, Martin	August 27, 1856	(Norway)
Hedstrom, Olaf	June 17, 1905	(Sweden)
Nelson, John	June, 1874	(Sweden)
Peterson, John	August 15, 1866	(Sweden)

THE SYRIANS

Tafeeda Maloly Bashara

Mary Maloley and unidentified male

Mary Maloley lived in Fort Wayne upon leaving Hartford City. No date on the photo; Mary was born in 1881 and died in 1944.

THE SYRIANS

Unlike many other immigrants who were displaced for religious, economic or political reasons, the Syrians came voluntarily and with the intention of returning home in two or three years much wealthier than when they came. And in most cases, they were not disappointed. The Syrians, as well as Greeks, Russians and other national groups, were lured to America by the notion of sudden wealth and the prestige it would confer on them and their families on their return home.

If wealth was his purpose, the Syrian immigrant's means to earn it was by peddling. As many as 95 percent arrived with the express purpose of peddling notions and dry goods. Men, as well as women and sometimes children, walked for miles through the country sides of every state selling their wares to isolated farmers and their wives who did not often get to town.

A heavy suitcase strapped to the back, a kashshi (box) fastened to the chest and a satchel in each hand was a typical portrait of the peddler. The packs contained many items including needles, pins, bright ribbons, fancy laces, embroidered pillow slips and table linens, and items of clothing, in some cases, even overalls and jackets. In some places the peddler was treated with disdain and contempt, in other places his visit was looked forward to with anticipation not only for the contents of the packs, but for the news he brought of the world farther away. Frequently, he was invited to share the family meal and given a bed for the night, and just as often, he was turned away.

Peddling reached its peak about 1895 to 1900, and began a slow decline about 1910 when the peddler's suitcase gave way to the retail shop.

The Syrians tended to immigrate in groups, sometimes whole villages. In America they continued to keep up relationships, living together in large houses or buildings. In the early 1890's Fort Wayne, Indiana, became a center for a large Syrian population. Hartford City also had several Syrian residents, perhaps as many as twelve or fifteen. The principal men were brothers, Salim and Kahlil Bashara. The Basharas were residents here in 1896, later moving to Fort Wayne where Salim was head of the colony there and became a man of wealth. He was noted for his astute business instincts, honesty and willingness to help his countrymen.

Following are items from local newspapers and other sources about the members of the Syrian colony which for fifteen years or so made Hartford City their home.

<u>Evening News</u>   February 17, 1896

Antonie LaBa and wife, Syrians, are very ill at the home of Joe LaBa on East Water Street. Antonie has a bad attack of typhoid fever and his wife has the lung fever.

<u>Evening News</u>   February 18, 1896

Antonie LaBa, a Syrian connected with the fruit trade in this city, died at the residence of his brother, Joseph, on East Waster Street at 9 o'clock last night of lung fever. His wife, who is also not expected to live, and one child survive him. Two weeks ago Mr. and Mrs. LaBa were taken sick with something like the grip. They had been in this country but a year and the climate was too rigorous. Their symptoms became worse and were aggravated by the fact that they refused to take medicine that was distasteful. Mrs. LaBa took a turn for the worse when she learned of her husband's death and it is not believed she will recover. (Antonie LaBa is buried on the east side of the Hartford City Cemetery)

<u>Evening News</u>   June 22, 1896

James, three-month old child of Joseph LaBa, the Syrian fruit dealer, died last evening of cholera infantum. The infant was buried this afternoon.

<u>Evening News</u>   August 5, 1896

Joe LaBa, the Syrian fruit dealer, got up at 5:00 o'clock this morning and when he looked over the family enrollment, he found one of his children missing. All the family were asleep and he could not account for the absence of the four year-old child. He looked about the premises and after the mother arose, she inquired over the neighborhood. Joe's brother was detailed on the case and he returned to the store without any news of the missing child. The family by this time had become much alarmed. It occurred to Joe that he ought to inspect all the closets and rooms about the house. He did so and found the little one in a closet fast asleep.

Telegram   August 5, 1896

Selim Bashara, the Syrian novelty dealer who occupies the crack in the wall east of Cooley's restaurant, is mourning the loss of a horse which disappeared so suddenly at the Middletown fair that Selim believes was stolen.

He was at the fair several days selling his wares and did a fairly good business. Friday morning he concluded to return to Hartford City and went out to get his horse. It was gone and Selim became much excited. He appealed to the big-hearted Marshal who personally offered to restore the horse to its owner for the paltry sum of $25. Selim has been in this country long enough to talk pretty fair English, and he understands the use of profanity. The Marshal made him so "red-headed" that he swore at him in Syrian, Greek, Belgian and English.

Another man came up at this juncture and suggested having some postal cards printed and sent over the country offering a reward for the stolen horse. Selim liked the idea and gave him a dollar to attend to the business. He never saw the man afterward or the dollar or the post cards.

The horse had cost but $25 and Selim did not propose to spend more than it was worth in order to regain him. He invested in another horse and came home. He interested several citizens at Middletown who promised to write him if the horse came their way. He is expecting a letter every day informing him that the animal has been recovered.

"What would I do with the robber?" said Selim, "I'd *!#*&%$#, that's what I'd do with him!"

Telegram   March 24, 1897

The Syrian population in this town in increasing. A boy baby was born to Joe LaBa, the south Jefferson Street fruit man and his wife.

Telegram   June 9, 1897

Thieves broke into Joe LaBa's fruit room in the basement of the Carrell building and stole $5 worth of fruit.

Telegram   June 30, 1897

The tarantula captured by Joe LaBa, the Syrian fruit dealer, on a bunch of bananas attracted a big crowd yesterday. Every now and then the handlers of fruit come across these ugly spiders and they quickly dispatch them. Joe came near being bitten before he discovered the venomous thing clinging to the fruit. It reached out for his hand, but the Syrian's quick eye caught sight of it just in time to escape being bitten. The bite is much dreaded by natives of countries where the tarantula is found. The bite produces a stupor and has been supposed to cause the disease called tarantism which is a mania for leaping and dancing, resembling St. Vitus dance.

Telegram   September 15, 1897

Joe LaBa, the Syrian fruit dealer, has moved to the South Side and will probably open a fruit store there.

Telegram   November 18, 1897

SANS SOUCI COLLAPSES

Sans Souci, formerly a popular South Side resort, collapsed Sunday night. The rear part of it was built on piles which were not set in the ground. The rain washed the earth from beneath the wooden pillars and they toppled over allowing the rear part of the building to settle down in a ravine.

Joe LaBa occupied the front part which rests on solid ground. His wife narrowly escaped going down with the part that collapsed. The rear part was occupied until recently by the Goosens and Burgess families who regard it lucky that they moved in time.

Sans Souci was once the center of South Side sporting life. The front part was a saloon while the rear was a big amphitheater in which sparring matches and dances were of frequent occurrence. The fencing in of the glass factory deprived the place of its prominence and lately it has been used as a tenement house.

<u>Telegram</u>   September 5, 1900

MIKE AND SILCAI

Monday afternoon about 4 o'clock Mike Isbal and Silcai Rizk, Syrians, formerly of Fort Wayne, were married at the Catholic Church. Father Dhe performed the ceremony in the presence of a few immediate friends.

The bridegroom was attended by his brother, George Izbal of Fort Wayne, and the bride by Mrs. Lizzie Bashara. After the wedding, the wedding party returned to the home of K. Bashara. A wedding supper was served at 7 o'clock. About fifteen Syrian people from Fort Wayne were present and they had a huge time.

The bride has only been in this country about two months. She met Izbal two weeks ago and it was a case of love on the spot. Silcai went to Fort Wayne to consult Mike's parents and see if she would be acceptable as a member of the family. The parents offered no objections, and Mike was willing. The bride is 16 and the groom is 20.

Mike took his bride on a wedding tour of the Madison County fair where they will sell fruit and have a good time. When they return they will make their home with K. Bashara and wife.

<u>Telegram</u>   May 29, 1900

K. Bashara, the enterprising fruit dealer, has a plan to establish a Syrian colony in this city. He is trying to make arrangements whereby forty Syrian families will take up residence on the South Side. This colony is only incidental to a wholesale notion store which Bashara wants to establish here. The store will be a supply depot for the Syrians who will all be engaged in peddling throughout the country. Bashara's brother has a similar store in Fort Wayne and he has grown wealthy in the business. The Syrians are successful peddlers and they take to the business as naturally as a duck to water. If Bashara's plans are carried out, the surrounding country will be overrun with vendors of notions and fruit, and the Syrian colony already here will be increased in numbers. The Syrians make good citizens and there will be no objection in this city to the growth of the colony.

<u>Evening News</u>   November 25, 1901

Selim Bashara, wife and two children of Fort Wayne, were yesterday the guests of Mr. Bashara's brother, K. Bashara, in this city. They came to attend the christening of two Syrian children at the Catholic Church. Selim Bashara is at the head of the Syrian colony in Fort Wayne.

<u>Evening News</u>   June 19, 1902

A WOMAN OF SYRIA

Mary Maloley leaves next month for Syria where she will spend a few months with her people and then return to this city. She will be remembered as the Syrian who carries two large black satchels around to the different cities about Hartford City and displays all kinds of dry goods. She has a trade that would be gratifying to most business men in the small towns and neither is it all cheap trade as is generally supposed of peddlers. In a satchel she carries several articles, bows and white goods, ranging in price up to $40. She does a credit business with people whom she thinks are good and has not lost an account up to this time, even now having an account with a woman in this town amounting to $85.

Since coming over to this country four years ago she has accumulated quite a little wealth for the old country and has become a very shrewd business woman. She has a mother, four sisters and a brother in Syria and her father died only last January in Jerusalem. She is not certain as to the cause of his death as all the mail is inspected by Turkish officials but she thinks that Turkey is responsible for it.

<u>Evening News</u>   June 24, 1903

THE SYRIANS

Although Hartford City has a considerable colony of Syrians, Fort Wayne is the center for this nationality in the west, and Selim Bashara, who is interested in this city, was until recently its undisputed head. The honor of Syrian leadership in this section is now divided between Bashara and Kaleel Teen, a younger man and a comparative newcomer.

Selim Bashara wandered into Fort Wayne fourteen years ago and opened a small store, in which he placed importations from Damascus,

Beirut and Constantinople, consisting of tapestries, laces and rare pieces of linen. Gradually American notions were added, and Bashara became a factor in Fort Wayne mercantile life. Other Syrians followed Bashara to Fort Wayne, and these he equipped with packs and started out to peddle among the country folk.

There are now between 225 and 250 Syrians in Fort Wayne. Most of these are men. The women are greatly in the minority, and there are less than a dozen Syrian children in the colony. The majority of the men are single, or have left wives in Syria while they struggle for an American fortune. The colonists do not live in cottages as Italians and other foreigners do. They prefer to rent large houses and live as one great family under one roof. The Syrians are clannish, and it is a noticeable fact that they occupy some of the largest houses in Fort Wayne. They make ideal flat dwellers.

Religion has an influence in the affairs of the Syrians in this section. The majority of them are Catholics, but the men who stand highest in the councils of the colony are Presbyterians. The Syrians do not allow religious prejudice to prevent their being sociable, and the Presbyterians willingly go to the Catholic Church when there is a Syrian feast day. The Catholics return the compliment when a Syrian missionary of the Presbyterian church comes among them.

The trade customs of the Syrians are peculiar. Saturday is their favorite trading day. The peddlers enter Fort Wayne after a journey through the country with their packs. They refill their packs on Saturday and on Monday board the trains leaving Fort Wayne and go forty, fifty and sometimes seventy-five miles into the country. Then they leave the train and walk back to Fort Wayne, selling their goods as they go. Many of them travel into Michigan. The women make the journeys as well as the men. They trudge mile after mile down the hot, dusty highways with great packs on their backs. Their only companion is a rude walking stick.

When the peddlers re-enter Fort Wayne they have sold their stock and bring back the money. The Syrians have not learned the soundness of American currency. They think paper money unstable and as soon as they reach Fort Wayne exchange it for gold. Each Syrian has a safety deposit box in one of the banks there and the gold is deposited there for safe-keeping. Almost every Saturday the peddlers who make the regular weekly trips to the bank, add gold to their pile and count over their money to feel assured that none is missing.

Some of the Syrian peddlers go out and stay out for months. When they return to the colony, they go to the bank accompanied by some of their countrymen who act as guards until the treasure is safely stowed away.

Several of the Syrians of Fort Wayne have returned to their native land since Selim Bashara began business there. They have made three or four thousand dollars and turned it into gold. When they go back to Damascus, or Beirut, they are called princes of fortune and are looked upon as millionaires. Selim Bashara and Kaleel Teen are both rich men and possessed of much American property. In old Syria they would pose as Pierpont Morgans and live in luxury.

Bashara owns several business blocks in Fort Wayne. Teen owns a splendid farm near the city.

<u>Evening News</u>   June 27, 1903

A SYRIAN FUNERAL

Mrs. Rosa Bashara died at the home of her son, Kaleem Bashara, in the Willman block, June 27, 1903. She was 64 years old and had suffered with heart trouble for some time. She had narrowly escaped death by suffocation two weeks earlier in a fire which destroyed their home on East Washington Street. While the immediate cause of her death was said to be heart trouble, it was thought that her end was hastened by the fire from which she was carried out from a sick bed almost dead from suffocation.

Mrs. Bashara was born in Beirut, Syria and came to this country in 1890 with her husband George. He died in 1900 and is buried in the Syrian graveyard in Fort Wayne. She leaves four sons, Charles and Selim of Fort Wayne, Kahlil of Hartford City and Said living in Brazil, South American, and one daughter, Selina, living in Syria.

Mrs. Bashara was highly regarded by the Syrians in this country and many attended her funeral at the Catholic Church. Grief over her death was felt in every town where there were Syrian dwellers. She was buried at the I. O. O. F. (Hartford City) cemetery.

A quaint, yet uncanny custom of the Syrians was to photograph their dead before burial. Usually the picture was taken of the corpse in the center of the group of the living. The photo was sent home to comfort the mourners in the old country. The living friends were pictured with the corpse in order to assure the folks at home that the dead was not without friends and comforters in his last moments.

Evening News   July 18, 1903

WILL MAKE A VISIT TO SYRIA

Mary Maloli (sic), the Syrian peddler who has been a familiar figure here for six years, will depart Monday afternoon on a trip to Syria. Mary came to this country seven years ago and started as a peddler at Fort Wayne. She has the natural shrewdness to make money and she has by hard work accumulated several hundred dollars which would be considered a small fortune in her country. Since she left home her father and other relatives have died and her mother wrote her some time ago that she wanted to see her daughter before she passed away.

Several Syrians of Fort Wayne will be here this evening to bid Mary adieu and send messages to their friends in their far away homes. Mary expects to return to Hartford City next spring and take up the work of peddling.

Evening News   October 28, 1903

MARY HADAD IS CLEAR OF NO. 3

Mary Hadad, the Syrian woman living at Montpelier, whose two bigamous marriages were mentioned in the Evening News last Saturday has dispensed with George Hadad, her third matrimonial acquisition, and is doing business on her own account. George turned over to Mary his fruit store and has gone to Fort Wayne.

Mary tells a Montpelier publication that she never was married to Mike Bashara, her first husband. She says she returned the marriage license and released young Mike before the ceremony was performed.

When Mary told her story to an Evening News reporter, not knowing he was a reporter, she claimed sympathy on the strength of the fact she had married Mike Bashara to get a home and Mike's brother tore him away from her. When she found she was talking to a reporter and not a lawyer she attempted to hedge and it seems she is still hedging at Montpelier.

Mary also told to a lawyer in Hartford City that she had been married to Mike Bashara.

<u>Blackford County Gazette</u>   October 31, 1903

George Hadad, who conducted the fruit stand here for some time, disposed of his store to his wife Saturday and left yesterday for Fort Wayne. George and his wife Mary Hadad, have agreed to disagree and in the future their ways will lead along widely diverging paths, says the <u>Montpelier Call</u>. It was stated that Mary had married Mike Bashara in Champaign, Illinois and had afterward married another man without getting a divorce. Mary denies this, says she never married Mike, but returned the marriage license and released him before the marriage was performed. She has obtained a clear title to the fruit store and will conduct it alone in the future.

<u>Evening News</u>   July 23, 1904

K. Bashara, the veteran fruit dealer, has sold his store on East Washington Street to George Litsfeld and Sam Michallis, who have come here from Fort Wayne to take charge of it. Mr. Bashara owns a novelty store on South Jefferson Street and has established a wholesale business with Syrian peddlers in the gas belt and will devote all of his time to the enlarging of that line of business.

<u>Evening News</u>   July 24, 1904

K. Bashara is in New York buying goods. Mr. Bashara has had a building erected next to his home at the corner of Cherry and Chestnut Streets and will occupy it along with the store now in the Interurban building. As most of Mr. Bashara's business is with Syrian peddlers at wholesale, he figures he can do as good business in his new location and save rent.

<u>Evening News</u>   December 19, 1904

SYRIANS WERE ROBBED EARLY

Sam Michallis, the Syrian who bought and now operates the fruit store in the Interurban building, some time ago decided to bring to this country friends of his in the old country who were to work for him on arrival. As they were people of his own country he sent them money with which to pay their passage across the ocean and their railroad fare to Hartford City.

The Syrians started but somewhere on the way a steamship agent convinced them that they had not enough money to pay their way and when the agent got through with them they had barely enough money to get back to Syria from the German point where they originally intended to take passage.

In due time came a letter from Syria to the Hartford City man informing him of the state of affairs. The Syrian here resolved to make sure the second time, and he purchased through Garvey and Berger, local travel agents, tickets which enabled his friends to travel from their home in Syria to this city and no dishonest agent can head them off.

It is said that robbing of untraveled foreigners bound for America is not an uncommon thing on the other side of the water. Usually however, the agents leave the emigrants enough money to get to New York. In the case of the Syrians they seem to have gone beyond the rule of robbery in their line.

Evening News   January 10, 1906

HAD HIS WIFE PUT IN JAIL

Mrs. Zeyton, wife of a Syrian peddler in this city, will be released from jail at Charleston, West Virginia, where she was placed along with her paramour, at the instance of her husband. Zeyton has come to the conclusion that it would cost too much to send the sheriff after the guilty couple and the money would be better expended in securing a divorce.

Zeyton came here from Fort Wayne some time ago and engaged in peddling, after the manner of his compatriots in this country. When he returned to Fort Wayne at intervals, stories came to his ears that connected his wife with another man, also a Syrian, in a way to arouse his suspicions. He then decided to remove his wife from the influence of the young Syrian and he brought her to this city.

The Fort Wayne Syrian followed and while Zeyton was out peddling he visited Mrs. Zeyton and induced her to elope with him. The couple fled to Charleston, West Virginia, where Zeyton has relatives. The latter informed him of the presence of his wife and her lover at Charleston and he brought about their arrest.

It was Zeyton's intention to send the sheriff with requisition papers after his wife and her lover and bring them back here for punishment. Tuesday morning Sheriff Hudson was getting ready to go to Indianapolis for the requisition papers when Zeyton changed his mind. He reasoned that if he got his wife back she would run away from him again and it would cost too much anyway. He announced that he would spend the money in securing a divorce. The West Virginia authorities will now turn the prisoners loose unless they want to prosecute them on their own account.

CHANGED HIS MIND WEDNESDAY

All the dark-skinned and black-orbed people who come to this country from Asiatic Turkey are not Turks nor Syrians nor yet Greeks. Many of them are Arabs. As these different nationalities speak pretty much the same language, they are inclined to fraternize in this country, although the Turk and the Arab are Mohammedans, while the Greek and Syrian are usually members of the Greek Catholic Church.

Zeyton, the peddler whose wife, ran away from him to land in jail at Charleston, West Virginia, is not a Syrian as was supposed. He is an Arab. He came from the same town in Syria that many of the Syrians here came from and naturally the Syrian colony here reminds him of home.

Simon Zeyton Tuesday was disposed to take the theft of his wife philosophically. He regretted the woman's downfall, but he declared it would be cheaper to get a divorce than it would be to get his wife back with no assurance that she would stay with him.

Wednesday morning Zeyton changed his mind. He went to Charleston to see his wife and probably take her back. The man with whom Mrs. Zeyton ran away is also an Arab.

Hartford City Daily Gazette   June 15, 1911

BIG FIRE NIPPED BY HEROIC WORK

Fire broke out Saturday afternoon in the old frame building on East Washington Street between Hiatt's bus barn and the McFerren grocery, and for a time threatened to do great damage.

The building was occupied by about twenty Syrians and one of them, an old woman, came near being burned alive. She was sick in bed. She was carried down a ladder almost suffocated with smoke. The heroic work of the firemen was all that saved the bus barn and the grocery. The roof of the barn caught fire but was easily put out. McFerren Brothers' grocery was not damaged by fire but the interior was ruined by water.

Salem Bashara states that he had $4000 worth of goods in the building. He has $1000 insurance.

Bashara also states that Sunday some boys and persons old enough to know better ransacked the partially destroyed building and carried away some goods. He says his wife had $50 in money, a gold watch and chain, and two gold rings taken from a trunk.

Two Syrians who resided in Blackford County in the 1900's were Mary Maloley and Tafeda Maloley Bashara.

Mary Maloley

Mary Maloley was part of the Syrian community in Hartford City, Indiana. She was a peddler and operator of a bawdy house and commonly known as "Dago Mary" while here. She certainly rose to become a leader in the Syrian community in Fort Wayne, Indiana.

While in Hartford City she dealt in diamonds and other jewels and evidently made enough money to go to Syria to get her niece Tafeda. Mary was 22 years old then and traveled alone to Beirut. She obviously learned the English language quickly and was able to "cut" a shrewd deal for she had a reputation here.

By 1908 Mary moved to Fort Wayne and became active in the affairs of that community. Men primarily dominated in the Syrian world, but Mary made connections and was able to gain the respect of the males and become a leader. There was no doubt that she knew how to make money and procure property, and she helped and guided many of her peers as they flourished in Fort Wayne. Mary, in physical terms, was a rather large woman and carried a purse with an alligator head on it (Alixa Naff, author of Arab Americans) Her stature and her money helped define her as a dominant person in the Allen County area and she was influential in the political arena as well. Mary never married but seemed to take care of everyone. Her nieces Nellie and Ginny Maloley related that she gave money for her nephews to start the Maloley Supermarkets in Fort Wayne. More than once Mary had legal charges brought against her, and it was stated that there had been a murder and Mary was somehow involved, but nothing ever came of this charge. It seemed that Mary had friends and acquaintances and connections throughout the Midwest. Mary died in Fort Wayne in December, 1944, and is buried in Lindenwood Cemetery.

(Personal interview with Nellie and Ginny Maloley sisters in Fort Wayne 2010).

Tafeda Maloley Bashara

Tafeda was just six years old when she left her home in Syria and came to America with her Aunt Mary Maloley. This was in November, 1903. Mary Maloley had been in Hartford City as part of a Syrian community that came during the Gas and Oil Days. Essentially this group were fruit dealers, peddlers, and shop owners.

Because Tafeda's mother had died and there was nobody left in their house except Tafeda and her father, Mary Maloley conjectured, "This girl is going to be in your way. Come, let me take her to America with me and my sister Sadie will bring her up." Tafeda's early reminiscences of her Aunt Mary were that she had made a lot of money peddling in America—"Ho! She was dressed and fixed and what—she was in her prime then and glory, you know, silk and ostrich feathers and diamonds and a watch pinned to her chest."

Well, after 30 days on a boat and arriving at Ellis Island, the two of them boarded a train for Hartford City, Indiana. "We got there just before Christmas. The lights were all lit. They took me downtown once. It was snowing—the snow was knee deep. They took me down to buy me a pair of leggings with buttons on them and an overcoat and a hat—a warm hat—warm clothes. And then is when I got my first glimpse of stores. The next day, second, and third and fourth, I found my own way back downtown and then I roamed the streets. I put my eye on one certain doll and a set of dishes in one of the store windows. I thought the possession of those two things would complete my life. And I'd go home and I'd say, 'Aunty, I saw dishes.' Anyhow they started talking about Santa Claus." Santa Claus coming down the chimney on Christmas was explained to Tafeda. She had seen his picture and were Santa Clauses on the corners of the square ringing bells. Christmas came. "We awakened from sleep, looked at the chimney. The fire was still burning." So her aunt sent her outside to see if the milkman had come. She went outside and found two boxes. Santa Claus had come! The big box contained the doll and the set of dishes was in the small box. "Well, my life was complete. There was nothing I wanted. It was all finished."

This was one of Tafeda Maloley's earliest memories as a young Syrian immigrant residing in Hartford City in 1903. In the spring of 1904 she started school. She did not know how to speak English. She admitted she had a lot of difficulty in school. "Everybody had to sit down, everybody had to stand. Be quiet." She spoke Arabic and not English so school was difficult for her.

Tafeda's story came from an audio tape made in 1963 by Alixa Naff. The transcribed version is in the archives at the Smithsonian American History Museum. (I visited there July 3, 2006 and photocopied the transcribed materials. These copies are available at the Blackford County Historical Society—Sinuard Castelo)

According to ellisislandrecords.org Mary Maloley and Tafeda Maloley arrived in New York on December 6, 1903. They traveled on the ship LaChampagne and departed from Havre. Tafeda was listed as six years old and Mary was 22. Assef Maloule (sic) (age 36), Tafeda's father came to America in 1912.

Daily Times Gazette   October 14, 1912

"DAGO" MARY HELD ON BLIND TIGER
CHARGE AT ANDERSON

Mary Maloley of Fort Wayne, known as "Dago" Mary through Northern Indiana, who recently settled in Anderson, was arrested, charged with operating a blind tiger. Four detectives surrounded the resort (house of prostitution) which the woman recently opened, and they say, she was in the act of selling quart bottles of liquor. She furnished a cash bond for her appearance in police court.

Hartford City News   December 18, 1922

FORMER SYRIAN WOMAN SOLD DIAMOND TO
THE SHAFFERS WHO OWED FOR THEM

Mary Maloley, the Syrian woman peddler who for years made her headquarters in Hartford City, and was a member of this city's little Syrian colony, figures in the Shaffer's murder mystery, in Henry County, as one to whom the Shaffers owed notes in payment for diamonds.

Mary Maloley moved from this city to Fort Wayne, Indiana, where she now resides. Soon after coming to this country she was shrewd enough to see the advantages of selling to women of the underworld. She got big prices, sold on payments, and as she accumulated money she invested in diamonds and jewelry, which she sold to the habitués of resorts at a large profit. Mrs. William G.Shaffer was at one time an inmate of a Muncie resort. Her husband was at one time a bartender. Both had a craze for diamonds and jewelry.

Mary Maloley did a big business in Muncie, in Hartford City and in fact throughout this section in the days when resorts flourished and wine and liquor flowed freely. She was wise enough to go out and in these resorts without spending much money herself. As a result she is reputed to be very wealthy. In fact no one knows just how much she is worth. She still continues to peddle, however, and always carries with her a large amount of jewelry.

That she has never been "bumped" off by some criminal who knows of the valuables she carries, has always been a mystery. But Mary is as strong as the strongest man and in an ordinary fray she could take care of herself.

A story illustrates her great strength is told of a traveling man who ran across Mary many years ago. Mary was carrying two large telescopes almost as large as trunks from the Lake Erie depot to her place on East Washington Street, in this city. She set the baggage down and was resting when the kind –hearted traveling salesman came by and offered to carry one of them. "All light," said Mary in her broken English, and she smiled from ear to ear as the traveling man tugged to lift the telescope. He could hardly raise it off the ground much less carry it. It was not "all light" but all heavy, too heavy for an ordinary man.

SYRIANS APPLYING FOR CITIZENSHIP IN BLACKFORD COUNTY

Name	Date of Arrival
Bashara, Mike	September 25, 1890
Emile, Charley	December 1, 1898
Seure, George	May 3, 1899

OTHERS APPLYING FOR CITIZENSHIP IN BLACKFORD COUNTY

Name	Date of Arrival	
Atso, Casto	February 15, 1914	(Macedonia)
Dineff, Tom	July 5, 1909	(Macedonia)
Glavas, Sam	May 15, 1905	(Macedonia)
Keremeleff, Spiro	April 25, 1913	(Macedonia)
Radeff, Apostol	July 20, 1913	(Macedonia)
Knossel, John	May 28, 1851	(Switzerland)
Waldvogle, Melchior	April 21, 1853	(Switzerland)
Pappas, Milt	August 12, 1906	(Turkey)

Plodding down the bricked Jefferson Street, a lone wagon driver passes by two men in front of the barber shop while a young lady appears to be looking into the Bank Saloon on quiet afternoon.